HAMPSHIRE
AT WAR 1939-45

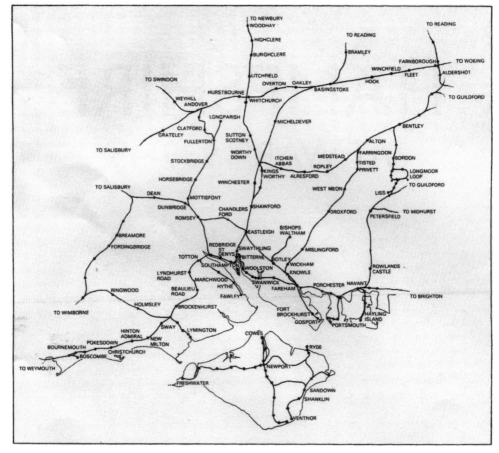

Hampshire's rail network in 1939.

YOUR TOWNS & CITIES IN WORLD WAR TWO

HAMPSHIRE
AT WAR 1939-45

MURRAY ROWLANDS

Pen & Sword
MILITARY

First published in Great Britain in 2018 by
PEN & SWORD MILITARY
An imprint of
Pen & Sword Books Ltd
Yorkshire – Philadelphia

ISBN 978 1 47386 9 967

Printed and bound in England by CPI Group (UK) Ltd, Croydon, CR0 4YY

Pen & Sword Books Limited incorporates the imprints of
Atlas, Archaeology, Aviation, Discovery, Family History, Fiction, History, Maritime, Military, Military Classics, Politics, Select, Transport, True Crime, Air World, Frontline Publishing, Leo Cooper, Remember When, Seaforth Publishing, The Praetorian Press, Wharncliffe Local History, Wharncliffe Transport, Wharncliffe True Crime and White Owl.

For a complete list of Pen & Sword titles please contact
PEN & SWORD BOOKS LIMITED
47 Church Street, Barnsley, South Yorkshire, S70 2AS, England
E-mail: enquiries@pen-and-sword.co.uk
Website: www.pen-and-sword.co.uk

or

PEN AND SWORD BOOKS
1950 Lawrence Rd, Havertown, PA 19083, USA
E-mail: Uspen-and-sword@casematepublishers.com
Website: www.penandswordbooks.com

Contents

Foreword and Acknowledgements

Writing a book covering the period of the Second World War in Hampshire and the Isle of Wight presented a major difficulty. This was because the county witnessed major events and played an important part in the war from Dunkirk to V-J Day. The reluctant move towards rearmament, the Phoney War, Dunkirk, the Battle of Britain, D-Day and VE Day have all been extensively anthologized. However, what was happening to Hampshire with people enduring the blitz and rationing while creating a platform for ultimate victory has been largely neglected. Creating a balance between a narrative of events during this period and describing each in human terms posed a major challenge. I hoped the key was to employ a wide range of commentators on wartime life between 1939 and 1945 so the monumental events of the war would become intelligible in human terms.

Special thanks are due to the Hampshire libraries, museums and archive centres visited by the author and their source material used in writing this book. The venues in question are individually listed within the Bibliography section (see 'Secondary Sources').

Much more than an editor: that was the role played by my wife Wendy in producing this book. At every stage at which difficult hurdles appeared, she was by my side suggesting ways in which they might be overcome. Therefore this book is as much hers as it is mine.

CHAPTER ONE

Hampshire: The Hub for any Defence of Britain

Any invasion of Britain would have to focus on Hampshire because of its geographical location. In 1939 Hampshire was much more than the geographical expression that it is now rapidly becoming. This automatically added to its vulnerability to any reduction in military spending which was a feature of Britain in the inter-war years. The dominant characteristic of these years was a reluctance to come to terms with the realities of total war as prefigured in 1936 by the Spanish Civil War. Joyce Carlisle, who lived on the outskirts of Southampton, is critical of the 'Britain can take it' view of civilian morale that has characterized the experience of months of bombing. Some indication of the consequences for civilian populations had been given by the Zeppelin attacks in the First World War. More than the reality for populations of being bombed by high explosives was the fear of gas attack which was assumed to be part of any new war. However, as the country slowly recovered from the Great Depression politicians such as Sir Eric Geddes were not prepared to countenance investment in defence, let alone the provision of shelters for those likely to be in direct line of attack from an invading force. The latter would come down to a mass-produced Anderson shelter or an improvised Morrison shelter built around the kitchen table in the final months when the British establishment finally confronted the reality of approaching war.

Hampshire had great strategic importance due to Portsmouth being a major base of the British navy. Around the city a whole range of activities relating to the navy took place, despite defence cuts. When belatedly serious thought began regarding the threat from Germany and how it might be countered following Hitler's acquisition of power in 1933, it was assumed that the kernel of defence of the realm would rest with the navy. Grudgingly, money was also made available for the development of new aircraft at Fairey Aviation, based at Southampton and Eastleigh as well as experimental work at Farnborough. Only reluctantly was Aldershot, the home of the British army, given the necessary finance for recruitment and exercises for the Territorial Army.

A recovery from the universal aversion to all things military that had arisen following the Great War slowly took place in the 1930s. Great faith

*Chamberlain. After the
Munich Agreement of 1938,
rearmament was halted in parts
of Hampshire.*

had been vested in the League of Nations
to retain peace. By the mid-1930s this
had been proved to be a false promise
by the actions of Italy and Germany that
had been left unchecked by appeasement.
This emphasized the mistaken belief
of the coalition government that an
expeditionary force would not be required
in the near future. Labour politicians such
as George Lansbury were reinforcing the
ideas of Conservative Treasury Ministers
who sought cuts in military expenditure.
Not until the mid-1930s was Lansbury
challenged by Labour's Ernest Bevin's call
for support of a rearmament programme.
The belief for much of the inter-war period
exemplified by Stanley Baldwin and
some other Tory politicians was that the
economic risk was greater than the military
threat facing the country. They accepted
there was a role for the military and that
was to protect Britain's imperial interests.
The navy's role in this was the protection
of mercantile interests. Because of this there was a reluctance to agree to the
construction of major capital ships which limited the development of aircraft
carriers, for instance, and adequate recognition of the crucial role that would
be played by submarines. A reflection of this can be seen in the struggle by
Portsmouth City Council to set up a seaplane base at Langstone Harbour
airbase. The council encountered repeated refusals from government to
fund the development, as well as a refusal to support a Bill in the House of
Commons backing the scheme. The minutes of Portsmouth Council in 1938
reflect its frustration with the Chamberlain government's intransigence over
this issue.

Neville Chamberlain's willingness to appease Hitler was reflected in
his inherent financial caution when he was elevated from Chancellor of
the Exchequer to prime minister in 1938. He said he could not accept the
demands of the military services for more spending. He complained:

> The country has been asked to maintain a larger army than it has for
> many years; a greater air force, which is a new arm altogether, and in
> addition, an army for use on the continent as well as facilities for the
> production of munitions which would be required not only by our forces
> but also our allies.

Even if Churchill had gained power prior to 1940 he would have experienced grave difficulties in moving beyond Chamberlain's more limited defence spending that had government and wider support. Just how much Chamberlain's belief that it might be possible to accommodate Hitler's demands was shared by political decision-makers in Hampshire is seen in the decision of Portsmouth Council to suspend some of its civil defence programmes in response to the Munich Agreement of 1938.

In relation to Portsmouth, government decision-making about the navy could be seen as having direct consequences for the city. A useful comparison is between spending on the navy in 1936 and that in 1914/15. In 1936 it was £18 million more than during the First World War, although there were only fifteen capital ships and none being built. By comparison in 1914/15 there were sixty-eight capital ships and fourteen being built. In 1936 the navy possessed only 54 battle-cruisers and 17 under construction, against 110 and 17 under construction in the previous era. The figures for destroyers were even worse: 54 and 12 being built as against 109 and 322. Bearing in mind the crucial role that submarines were to play in the Second World War, the navy only possessed fifty-one compared with seventy-four in the First World War when they were a relatively new naval development.

The rivalry between the navy and the Air Force was reflected not only over the proposed Langstone Base but also other bases around Portsmouth in relation to the operation of seaborne aircraft. In a speech on 18 March 1936 Churchill, who had just been brought in as First Lord of the Admiralty, said 'The foundation of British Navy policy is the acceptance of the principle of parity with the United States not only in battleships but over the whole range of the Fleet.' Despite America being determinedly isolationist, Churchill saw America as an ally exemplified by the thousands of American troops in Hampshire prior to D-Day. It is interesting that Churchill had to justify the construction of aircraft carriers through their role in protecting trade. The Defence Requirements Subcommittee of the House of Commons finally advocated that the strength of the British navy should be equivalent to that of the combined Japanese and German navies; a radical departure from attempts to commit the size of the navy based on international agreement. Unfortunately, even in 1937 the gain of the Fleet Air Arm by the navy from the Air Force came too late for its requirement of modern planes prior to the outbreak of war. However, by 1939 Portsmouth dockyards were part of a record ship-building programme involving the construction of 200 vessels or 870,000 tons of new shipping. By 1940/41 the output from British dockyards including Portsmouth had at last exceeded that for a comparable period in the Great War. Portsmouth's dockyards were making a major contribution towards updating the existing fleet through the installation of anti-aircraft (AA) guns and more accurate systems of control. From 1936 the number of systems capable of firing a shell of 2lb had risen by 75 per cent.

Aldershot certainly was not immune from the cuts in defence spending made following the First World War for whom the spearhead was Sir Eric Geddes. The only corps formed during the war to survive was the Royal Tank Corps. Others such as the Machine-Gun Corps were disbanded and their function subsumed within infantry units. In 1920 the Royal Signals was created, moving it out of the Royal Engineers. Sir Douglas Haig's beloved sixteen cavalry units were reduced from sixteen to eight with big reductions to the infantry battalions and size of the Territorial force. When the Irish Free State was created in 1922, six Irish regiments were lost from the British army. Despite this, many Irish soldiers serving in Aldershot decided to stay with regiments based in the town. Regiments would periodically return to Aldershot, filling gaps in their main role as imperial policemen. Until the mid-1930s army life in Aldershot was characterized by military tattoos rather than encouragement from top brass of experimental work such as that related to the Experimental Mechanical Force through the REME in 1927–28. Worse still, the army failed to make its case for rearmament in competition with the

Military tattoos dominated the life of Aldershot, home of the British army between the two world wars.

navy and Air Force. It was not until the Munich Crisis of 1938 that serious moves were made to expand the army to a realistic level by increasing the size of the Territorial Army and the reintroduction of conscription in April of the following year. By mid-1939 the British army consisted of 230,000 regulars and 453,000 Territorials and reservists. This was dwarfed by the German army who, under the guise of labour battalions and glider instruction, had got around the restrictions of the Treaty of Versailles that placed limitations on recreating a large army. Some progress was made, however, through the creation of the Auxiliary Territorial Service for women, enabling men to be released for front-line service, something that accelerated in 1940.

Research from contemporary reports from papers written on the cusp of war reveals the unreadiness of Britain for a German attack. There was a deficiency of trained officers. The provision of barracks for the army was well below the safety line. Troops would arrive after mobilization without any provision being made for their physical support. No system existed within the Southern Command for the obtaining of appropriate supplies, nor was there any identified person to order these supplies. The NAAFI was woefully unprepared for a total war situation. The consequence of local commanders ordering locally caused shortages within the areas surrounding southern camps. The Territorials arriving at their barracks were on subsistence rations for fourteen days. The vital organization of petrol supplies was lacking. Low pay for barrack wardens drawn from retired officers resulted in these men seeking other employment. Because of the absence of effective systems, chaotic issuing of uniforms and stores took place without an adequate audit. There was a history of weak liaison with Territorial groups that resulted in men arriving at barracks without a central direction and adequate preparation being made for their arrival. With experienced staff from the regular army being mobilized, there was a void of army officers capable of offering training; this resulted in substandard training being available to Territorials and volunteers. The vehicles taken over by the army from civilians were not fit for military use. Mobilization could result in a highly-qualified military engineer being placed in charge of military baking.

Evidence from the Buller Barracks in Aldershot reveals that even in peacetime the Royal Army Ordnance Corps struggled to adequately supply the services and materials that were part of its brief. There was a desperate shortage of trained drivers as well as a whole range of tradesmen. Upon mobilization, regular soldiers' positions were filled by members of the Territorial Army but there was no like-for-like acquisition of necessary skills in the changeover. Urgent questions relating to the possession of craft skills had to be given to the militia men pouring into Aldershot, sometimes as many as 400 in each train. There was a desperate shortage of accommodation, with mobilized men sleeping in sheds, gyms, the riding school and the drill hall. In the search for tradesmen it was found that a 'fitter' referred to a fitter of corsets! The War Office wrote on 19 December 1939 complaining about commanding officers awarding commissions to friends in a desperate move to acquire senior staff.

A grim picture of the British army post-First World War as the result of financial constraints can be seen. Officers in Aldershot were distinguished by their preoccupation with hunting and spending six times as much on cavalry training as training with tanks. The army was starved of money, consigning its men to leaking huts with uncomfortable iron beds. The food offered featured greasy porridge, rissoles, and dry bread washed down with sweetened cocoa. The two shillings paid per day were in real terms less than soldiers had been paid at Waterloo. It was said of the officers that they travelled the world to hot spots such as Palestine in 1936 without learning anything about the countries in which they served. Hopes were expressed that officers training at Sandhurst might be roughly up to the standard of West Point in America but these were dashed through lack of funding. Even after the expansion of the Territorials in 1936, they suffered through lack of equipment. In April 1939 the decision was made to double Hampshire's Territorial Army and, using existing drill halls throughout the county, recruitment began. At Merry Oak, Bitterne near Southampton, A Company was formed; B Company at Carlton Place, Southampton; C Company at Holdenhurst Road, Bournemouth and Portfield Road at Christchurch. Platoons formed up in Bath Road, Lymington and in Fordingbridge. As recruits poured in, raising the total strength to 1,250, new drill stations opened at Swanwick, Botley, New Milton and Brockenhurst. Permanent staff instructors were appointed to the expanding battalion, which by August had almost achieved two-battalion status. However, the war history of the 7th Battalion Hampshire Regiment, above a photo of the Hampshire Regiment's annual camp, talks of the unpreparedness of the military situation on the eve of war.

The first and second infantry battalions were based in Aldershot. They formed the spearhead corps available for deployment abroad. There were only two brigades of anti-aircraft artillery alongside some belated mechanization. From 1932 anti-aircraft provision was made in the Territorial Army and this increased from 1935 alongside slow mechanization of the cavalry units.

As far as the Air Force was concerned, the interwar period was 'up in the air' until the prospect of war appeared on the horizon. In 1917 there were seventy-three aerodromes operating in Britain. In just one year this had been expanded to 301, but by 1924 the number of aerodromes had dropped to 44 comprising 27 military and 17 civilian. By contrast, although the Germans had lost the Great War, by 1930 they had begun a whole process of aircraft expansion. The British response to this poorly-disguised German activity was to further cut its aircraft expenditure, reducing Britain's position as top air power in 1918 to fifth in 1933. However, from 1934 there was a belated recognition of the threat posed by German air development and the Royal Air

Force (RAF) was increased by forty-one squadrons. Farnborough renewed its work in testing new aircraft designs. Air training took place at Hamble Worth giving cadets an experience of flying, and also a home for Fairey Aviation who played a major role in aircraft manufacture.

In Alan Cobham's work for aviation can be seen something that raised the whole consciousness of the vital role which the development of the aircraft industry would play in the future of Britain. Arriving in Eastleigh in August 1936, he began the process of developing a commercial aerodrome that was to play a crucial role in developing the Spitfire when Supermarine used it for test flying. It came to be called Southampton Airport and became an invaluable location for RAF squadrons holding summer camps. This coincided with Supermarine's work on a desperately-needed single-seater fighter that was created by their chief designer R.J. Mitchell and appropriately named the Spitfire. By June 1936 the RAF had ordered 310 of these and Supermarine commenced their construction alongside amphibious flying boats. The first Spitfire was not available to fly until 15 May 1938 and entered service with 19 Squadron of the RAF in August 1938. However, producing an adequate number of Spitfires proved difficult so that by the beginning of 1939 only forty-nine had been delivered. There was a menacing comparison with Luftwaffe Fighter Command and although Hawker Hurricanes were being delivered to the RAF, Britain lacked the aircraft for adequate defence. In April 1938 the Air Ministry took control of air traffic facilities with civil aviation terminating in early 1939. There was a rush to camouflage the buildings at Eastleigh as war approached but how effective this was against massed attack in 1940 is open to question.

In 1921 the Royal Aircraft Establishment (RAE) at Farnborough had absorbed the Instrument Design Establishment based at Biggin Hill and the Air Ministry's Air Worthiness Department. Despite cutbacks elsewhere, no expense was spared in a whole range of activities including testing and research work on aircraft engines, flight refuelling and flying at high altitudes. Farnborough was renowned for its wind tunnel. As an indication of the importance that air defence was about to play, the Anti-Aircraft Co-op Unit was based here alongside the School of Photography. The RAE was to play an absolutely crucial role in the testing of German aircraft when they fell into British hands.

Lee-on-Solent was important in providing a link between air and naval activity. In 1920 it was renamed as the School for Naval Co-Operation and in 1939 was taken over by the Admiralty as HMS *Daedalus* airfield. It played a crucial role in training seaplane pilots. Supermarine built 287 planes including the Swordfish for aircraft carriers as part of a programme of amphibious aircraft construction. Odiham's expansion in the early 1930s owed much to its strategic proximity to Aldershot and Farnborough and by 1936 No. 4 Squadron had moved across from Farnborough to the new base.

Because its grass runway was unsuitable for heavy bombing aircraft it was the first airfield in the south-east to receive a concrete runway.

Despite an overall policy of appeasement, priority was given to the development of a system of air defence with the reality of the Spanish Civil War underlining the need for civilian protection. The Home Chain system of radar was developed in top secret, together with the creation of two planes for fighter defence: the Hurricane and the Spitfire. The Spitfire Type 300 prototype made its maiden flight from Eastleigh Airport on 5 March 1936. Vickers Armstrong Ltd used Eastleigh for flight testing. The decision taken in 1937 to press ahead with production of these aircraft was the vital factor of victory in the Battle of Britain in 1940. An example of just one of the many bases opened for the Air Force and which played a crucial role throughout the war is that of Calshot in the New Forest. It opened as a Naval Air Station in 1911 and seaplanes used its spit for access onto Southampton Water. Between the wars it had been a training station and was renamed RAF Calshot. It had also been a major base for the Schneider Cup races of 1929 and 1931 which provided an invaluable basis for testing the capabilities of new aircraft.

J. Laing, constructing Hampshire's airfields.

Conning towers built by J. Laing.

In August 1939, 600 Territorials arrived at the New Forest from Waterloo as part of a training exercise. Unfortunately bad weather washed out much of the training, despite billeting being arranged in schools at Lymington, Beaulieu, Boldre and East Boldre. Appeals went out for volunteers for air-raid precaution (ARP) training that included dispatch riders and boy runners. There was a mock air-raid in Lymington in June and the New Forest participated in the blackout exercise covering the south of England. Brockenhurst Station was in constant use, providing easy access to the Forest's military camps, while Holmsley Station began to develop a major role as a dispersal centre. Eventually every man, woman and child was in possession of a gas mask. However, the removal of road signs caused considerable confusion as there were still a large number of holidaymakers in the New Forest. Like millions of other people around the country, people here were learning how to use stirrup pumps and cope with incendiary bombs. Bob Dowling from Fordingbridge was scathing about the exercises in which his group of volunteers was involved:

> They used a civilian car as a German tank. We had to just use tin cans of gravel as make-believe hand grenades. We had to run out alongside the car and throw our cans on the roof. The chances are that a real tank crew would have machine-gunned us.

CHAPTER TWO

How the Civilian Population Prepared for War

It should be remembered that in the 1930s very few people possessed cars or telephones so communications and mobility were extremely limited in comparison with today. When councils in Hampshire began to be required to provide protection for their communities, this was focused in identifiable suburbs and villages. Until it became apparent that the Germans were not intending to mount a gas attack on Britain in the first months of the war, there was still an assumption that gas would be employed by them. Within the Air-Raid Precautions Act considerable attention was devoted to gas attack and how to prepare for it. Councils were required to appoint an air-raid precautions officer and a great part of this work revolved around a gas attack. Faced with the terrible dangers in prospect exemplified by the Spanish Civil War, people refused to believe that war was inevitable and after Chamberlain's negotiations in Munich it was thought that peace had been agreed 'in our time' when it was merely a breathing space before the certain reality of hostilities. Perhaps this is why for most of Hampshire there were never enough public shelters in Portsmouth or Southampton and a rush occurred to provide Anderson shelters for people's gardens, later supplemented by the indoor Morrison shelters. It has been commented that German shelters were generally considered superior to their British counterparts.

It was recognized that because there would be insufficient time to reach shelters covering the needs of a number of streets, those who could afford it should be encouraged to build their own shelters. Certainly at the start of the war it was a case of households seeking to arrange their own shelters, even if it was only the Morrison version of a converted table. It should be noted how this effectively discriminated against the poorest who lacked the funds needed to build more effective shelters for themselves. Many Hampshire families never went to the few public shelters provided. Difficulties arose in the areas where inadequate services were faced with responding to overwhelming air-raids. Despite the pre-war Fire Brigade Act, at the peak of the blitz the fire service was stretched to breaking-point in Southampton, Portsmouth and Gosport, support being provided from other parts of Hampshire and even Wiltshire. A question might be asked about whether the crisis in the water supply might have been avoided at the peak of the blitz in Portsmouth when no water was available to fire-fighters.

Authorities such as Portsmouth were required to respond to directives coming from government and coordinated by Hampshire County Council beginning in April 1935 with a Home Office directive on coping with air-raids, followed by the Air-Raid Precautions Act in 1937 and finance being made available to boost fire-fighting services in the following year. Practical support included a £3 grant for each auxiliary fireman employed, together with support for sixty hours of training. Categories for the employment of the community in civic defence were created involving men and women aged from 16 to 50. Despite this, in Hampshire there was criticism of the equipment available to meet a threat of this dimension, leading to the government responding with the Fire Brigades Act of 1938 and the ordering of 5,774 new pumps and 1,100 miles of pipe. In the case of Portsmouth this resulted in the receipt of thirty-five additional pumps, sixty-four towing vehicles and 30,000ft of new hose in February 1939. Supporting this was a fleet of flatbed lorries, conscripted bakers' vans, taxis and private cars capable of towing pumps. It became apparent that women would have to be employed, as men were conscripted into the armed services. We shall see how this forward planning helped in coping with the extreme test faced by the fire service in Portsmouth.

In the air No. 10 and 11 Groups were given operational control of southern airfields including Hampshire. Air Chief Marshal Hugh Dowding suggested that forty-five fighter battalions would be necessary to defend the country. Out of a total number of 759 fighters, only 93 were the newly-acquired Hurricanes. Until 1939, air-traffic control had been minimal but work towards an early-warning system had commenced in the 1920s with the construction of sound mirrors. Then the Scientific Survey of Air Defence received proposals from Watson-Watt for equipment and location which were followed up in 1936 and towers were erected including one at Ventnor on the Isle of Wight. The construction of radar towers along the south coast was held up by landowners and land had to be compulsorily purchased. At Ventnor a 360ft steel tower was built with the power supply coming from the national grid backed up by a stand-by generator. By 1939 all twenty radar stations were working and came to be protected by members of the RAF Regiment. However, it was soon discovered that low-flying aircraft could avoid detection and although stations were built in Sussex and Dorset, none were built in Hampshire. Portsmouth, Gosport and Southampton – which suffered raids from low-flying Luftwaffe aircraft – paid dearly for this oversight. Crucially, the system was backed by the Observer Corps usually sited close to telephone exchanges. Hampshire was No. 3 Group in the Royal Observer Corps with its base in Winchester. It had forty-eight outside posts.

Women increasingly dominated work in aircraft production.

The Women's Royal Army Corps (WRAC) raising consciousness of the need for preparation for war.

Strategic roads in Hampshire were closed to traffic.

The Cunliffe-Owen factory at Eastleigh.

Production of the Spitfire.

*Gracie Fields at the helm of the Isle
of Wight paddle-steamer the* Gracie
Fields, *sunk at Dunkirk in 1940.*

CHAPTER THREE

War Approaches

In January 1939 Lord Wolmer, MP for Aldershot, spoke at the garrison town's Conservative Club. Although the gloss had clearly come off the Munich Agreement of the previous year, by then he was still concerned to give credit to Prime Minister Chamberlain, describing he and Churchill as 'two remarkable men'. He did, however, concede that every nation in Europe was now furiously rearming and claimed that the warm welcome the prime minister had received on a recent visit to Mussolini's Italy indicated the desire for peace between the two countries. While denying any assistance to the struggling Spanish government under attack from Franco, he claimed that Britain's defences were in an 'impregnable state'. In a speech in Hartley Wintney on 20 January he was calling for higher production levels of armaments. He went on to welcome the appointment of Sir John Anderson who had been given responsibility for national air-raid protection.

Regarding planning of how to deal with mass air attacks on cities and built-up urban areas within Hampshire, the question began to arise as to whether Aldershot and Farnborough were areas from which children should be evacuated or whether they should take evacuees themselves. If they were seen as neutral areas the Aldershot town clerk said that work would have to be done to ascertain how many evacuees each house should accept. At the start of a town football match at the Aldershot ground an appeal for ARP personnel was made by the town clerk: 'The outstanding vacancy is for male volunteers and a special appeal is made for men who wish to undertake this noble service.' He went on to say that air-raid wardens were particularly needed in North Camp, Ash Road and the centre of Aldershot. Aldershot and Farnborough and all the surrounding areas were seeking to respond to Chamberlain's radio appeal for a national system of volunteers to enable the country to cope with total war. As far as evacuees were concerned, the mayor of Aldershot had sought the town's teachers' help as enumerators to identify the space in houses capable of accommodating evacuees. Meanwhile in nearby Fleet a census of suitable available space had already been taken.

By February 1939 air-raid wardens in Aldershot were expressing concern about the slow progress of ARP organization. They had neither been given the work they felt they should do nor indeed any indication of what they should be doing. Problems had arisen over the distribution of respirators in the event of gas attacks. The chief warden indicated that for Aldershot

The call-up of Territorials to Aldershot in 1939.

A gas-masked ARP assists children.

about 600 wardens would be required and that they should spend time getting to know the residents in each of their sectors, and because the town had a rapidly-changing population, also be aware of comings and goings. Major A.S. Dundas, the chief air-raid warden, stated that checks had to be made to ensure that each of their households had been supplied with a respirator. Further training in first aid and ways to cope with incendiary bombs would be provided. In Fleet the chairman of Fleet Urban District Council was bitter in his criticism of Hampshire County Council because of delays in ARP planning and resourcing. In a letter of 1 August, Captain C.G. Mathew J.P. complained that the date by which Fleet would have its ARP preparation completed was continually having to be revised. In July the council had reported serious delays in the construction of shelters. In Cove and Farnborough a rehearsal showed a lack of coordination between the siren warnings with the one in Cove itself failing to work at all.

Meanwhile Aldershot Council had ordered 100 auxiliary firemen's uniforms and discovered that the main siren for the air-raid alarm failed to work. In frustration it passed responsibility for the elimination of street lighting back to Hampshire County Council. The mayor expressed his concerns at the delays in organizing the ARP in Aldershot. In Farnborough the council was discussing how to manage the provision of billeting members of the armed forces in the town and the council moved to carry out a survey of accommodation that might be available. By 10 March 1939 a meeting of 300 air-raid wardens, fire brigades and auxiliary firemen from Aldershot, Farnborough, Odiham and the surrounding area were given a demonstration of how to cope with an incendiary bomb. It was unfortunately reported that essential equipment had not been received by the council so a follow-up exercise scheduled for Sunday, 26 March could not take place. Farnborough Council decided to purchase four air-raid shelters at a cost of £160 on a trial basis in preparation for the development of a more comprehensive scheme of shelters. These would be for people on the street at the time of an air-raid and for use at council depots.

Lord Wolmer, the town's MP, was again speaking at the Conservative Club. He now confirmed that many in the Conservative government had been 'kidding themselves' when they believed that the Munich Agreement represented any real hope of peace in Europe. Yet with somewhat distorted logic he was still able to refer to Chamberlain, the architect of appeasement, as making 'a great speech' in Birmingham the week before. While deploring the consequence of appeasement in signing away one of the best armies in Europe, that of the Czechs, Lord Wolmer still gave his support to Lord Halifax, a supporter of appeasement. At the same time, for Aldershot ears he was critical of the pace of rearmament. He was making this speech ahead of a major blackout exercise covering not only Hampshire but also Surrey and Berkshire on 6 May. Before this, passive air-raid precautions took place over 60 square miles to test warning systems and the capability of dealing with gas, incendiary and high-explosive bombs. Demonstrations attended by Mayor A.J. Stroud in Aldershot were given featuring the use of rattles when mustard gas and high-explosive (HE) bombs were dropped. The *Aldershot News* then described how the Aldershot Command was completely blacked out on 6 May, together with RAF stations at Farnborough and Odiham. Pilots from the RAF then tested its effectiveness and indicated they were unable to distinguish one part of the command from another. In the barracks total blackout began at 9 pm and passive air defence equipment was tested. It was reported that the exercise was made more effective by dense fog. Incidents were staged at Aldershot and Farnborough involving ARP personnel and fire-fighters. For both councils the fire brigades dealt with real fires.

With the announcement of national conscription in May 1939, the columns of the *Aldershot News* carried a fierce debate about the merits of conscientious objection. Johnston-Martin, the minister of Aldershot Presbyterian Church, deplored the way in which Chamberlain had gone back on his word; a promise made earlier in the year not to reintroduce conscription. He deplored the way in which the proposed Bill was introducing elements of religious intolerance and giving Christians Hobson's choice in relation to serving in the armed forces or even being involved in defence-related work such as ARP volunteering. According to the Reverend Johnston-Martin, a Christian pacifist is not a coward if he maintains his belief while others are serving their county abroad and putting their lives at risk on his behalf. In his sermon he warned of the war-mindedness that followed from elaborate measures for defence then being introduced. In response, the Aldershot British Legion branch secretary wrote deploring the use of the phrase 'wholesale murderers' to describe serving soldiers. It was 'not worthy of one who professes Christianity.' A mother of three sons who were all likely to be called up joined in the criticism of the minister, saying that her definition of conscientious objection amounted to cowardice. The Reverend G.W.N. Archer brought the issue down to the fundamental question of whether war could ever be justified at all, in a similar way that it had in Aldershot in the First World War.

Events were rapidly overtaking philosophical discussions of this kind. Speaking to Conservatives in Fleet, Lord Wolmer outlined how assurances of military support had been given to Poland, Turkey and Romania by Chamberlain on the basis of the superior military strength enjoyed by Britain, France and Poland. He gave an unconvincing analysis of the vulnerability of the Nazi regime to pressures from the Catholic Church, socialists and business interests within Germany. In the meantime, hard practical planning for enemy attack guided by the senior ARP officer had identified public shelters in a number of places in Aldershot. A place for training purposes with incendiary bombs was identified, together with somewhere where decontamination could take place following a gas attack. This involved a concrete platform 40ft by 30ft with an adequate supply of water and drainage. Measures were taken to ensure that the fire station was adequately protected and the original fire siren supplied by Hampshire County Council was replaced with one to be located at the gas works. On 11 August Aldershot was involved in an exercise covering more than half of England involving a blackout on 10 August through till 4 am on 12 August. A total of 1,300 aircraft participated and the objective was to prepare for an attack that was to come within months. There were 800 defending fighters and these fighters had to make the maximum number of interceptions against invading aircraft. These comprised 500 bombers: Wellingtons, Hampdens, Whitleys and Blenheims operating from bases in France.

This coincided with the arrival of several thousand of the 34,000 men of the militia called up for training in Aldershot from the end of July into August. The army had taken moves to welcome their 'guests' by laying on lorries and buses supervised by military policemen with megaphones. Whether it was a tongue-in-cheek observation from the *News*, it reported that the officers and NCOs were greeted 'as though they were their own sons.' We are given an image of the men who were to make up the Expeditionary Force sent to France a few weeks later: 'Many of the men were bare-headed and sports coats and flannels seemed to be the most popular dress.' The suggestion that the social class divide of the previous war may have changed was given by the arrival of a chauffeur-driven Rolls Royce from which the militia man walked to join his comrades in the waiting lorries.

At nearby Fleet Station men for the RAMC and RASC arrived to make their short journey to Crookham Camp. Among their number there were no infantrymen because they had been consigned to two months' training in regimental barracks. These men had come from all over the country and some had travelled all night. For one of the men there was disappointment for he had brought his bride of a week expecting army accommodation. Being disappointed, he went off to find a room outside barracks. The routine in camp consisted of supplying the men with necessary personal effects, a welcome meal and exchanging their civilian clothes for army kit. Battledress, consistent with that of the regular army, was a cap, canvas clothing, underclothes, shirts, boots and a pair of canvas shoes. Boyce Barracks at Crookham, the first purpose-built militia barracks which had only existed since 1 May, was now occupied by 900 militia men and training staff. On the following day Lieutenant General Sir John Dill visited the RASC camp and on the following day visited the camp at Arborfield where instruction on anti-aircraft guns was taking place.

Within days of the outbreak of war there was evidence of growing consciousness of its implications for Hampshire. Local cinemas were showing *The Warning* which portrayed the reality of an air-raid. The *Aldershot News* at the beginning of September published a letter from Robert Maine both appealing for volunteers and seeking to make the residents of Aldershot and the surrounding area aware of the implication of air-raids. It was every resident's duty to be aware of what was required of them as outlined in Public Information Leaflet Number 1 dealing with air-raid warnings, gas masks, lighting restrictions, fire precautions, evacuations and food. On 1 September the archbishops of Canterbury and Westminster published an intercession for peace for both Anglicans and Catholics. Despite difficulty in obtaining sites, Aldershot Council was able to publish a list of fifteen shelters and first-aid posts. The local Women's Voluntary Service (WVS) issued an appeal for women between the ages of 17 and 65 to volunteer as wardens, ambulance drivers, owner drivers, nursing auxiliaries, canteen workers in both Aldershot town and the military camp, hospital supply workers, clerks, telephonists and messengers and assisting with blood banks. When the news came that the Germans had invaded Poland, instructions were given to evacuate Aldershot Hospital for use as a casualty clearing station. Volunteers were busy reinforcing the hospital's walls with sandbags. Details of the billeting arrangements for troops from the Dominions were published, allowing 10d a night for the first soldier and 8d a night for each additional soldier. Breakfast consisted of 5oz of bread, 1oz of butter, 1 pint of tea with milk and sugar, 4oz of bacon, and 1oz of marmalade was costed at 8d. Dinner consisted of 10oz of meat, 3oz of bread, 10oz of potatoes, 8oz of vegetables and 4oz of pudding was costed at 11d. Tea comprised 4oz of bread, ½oz of margarine, 1 pint of tea with milk and sugar and 2oz of jam was costed at 3d. Supper was 3oz of bread and 1 pint of tea with milk and sugar, and 4oz of meat was costed at 5d.

Amid all the anxiety and depression associated with the war, the military show in Aldershot provided some relief. It was called *Don't be Rough, Sergeant* with Private Scrounger, *La Desire* (a sensational dance number), the Sun-Kissed Peach Girls and a famous BBC trio. The presence of the Royal Artillery Mounted Band provided concerts at the Royal Artillery Officers' Mess at Wellington Barracks. The concert included music by Mendelssohn, Grieg, Smetana and Saint-Saëns.

Symptomatic of the sacrifice some Hampshire families were prepared to make in terms of their war effort were the Holbrooks. The family closed their house in London and moved down to Weston Patrick near Basingstoke. All three sons of Sir Arthur Holbrook had been called up, joining Lieutenant Alec W. Holbrook MC and Major W. Holbrook who were already serving in the armed forces. Tim Childerhouse – a former librarian at Aldershot Library who produced the picture book *Bygone Aldershot* – described, as a young man, what life was like in Aldershot in the months leading up to the war. Trains arrived regularly at Aldershot Station carrying contractors working on the barracks hastily being constructed in the camp. There was continual movement with the regular army being placed in billets so that the territorials could occupy their barracks during training. The flamboyant church parades along Queen's Avenue became a thing of the past as eyes turned skyward to watch the new Spitfires and Hurricanes being tested at Farnborough. Childerhouse took advantage of the government-subsidized pilot training scheme at 2s and 6d an hour and noted a greater willingness on the part of employers to allow all Territorial soldiers fifteen to twenty days each year for training. Just when Aldershot Town's manager, Joe McCracken, had secured regular good performances in Division 3, the declaration of war was accompanied by a ban on professional football.

There was clearly a tactical mistake made by the government in not recognizing that the Isle of Wight's proximity to Portsmouth made it uniquely vulnerable to attack. There was some recognition of this, however, with the formation of an ARP group for Ryde and Bembridge in March 1939 and active participation in the regional blackout exercise. The island's industry of shipbuilding and aircraft production was not initially recognized as being in need of protection.

Astride a new tank.

CHAPTER FOUR

Evacuation: Saving Hampshire's Children

Let us start with the dictionary definition of evacuation: 'To withdraw or cause to withdraw from a place of danger to a place of greater safety.' In April 1939 Southampton Council issued instructions that children be prepared to evacuate with gas masks, underclothes, day and night clothes, house shoes, stocking/socks, toothbrush, knife, fork, spoons, mug, plate, comb, towel and handkerchiefs. The first British evacuation in September 1939 was the largest mass movement of people ever seen in Britain. The government's reasons for initiating the evacuation was prompted by a fear that mass bombing would result in a collapse of civilian morale. The task was to identify neutral areas capable of accepting large numbers of children and, for children below the age of 5, their mothers as well. The order for evacuation came into being on 1 September 1939. Previously letters to parents had gone out in Southampton urging parents to take advantage of council schemes to move their children to the countryside from crowded vulnerable areas and urging them to register for a place. Meetings were held at schools where head teachers charged with detailed plans explained what would happen. Most Southampton children went to North Hampshire or Dorset with teachers accompanying their classes in the hope that teaching could continue. Attempts were made to keep siblings together; if not in the same house, then close enough for parents to conveniently visit both.

The country had been split into three areas for evacuation: the key industrial cities where attacks were expected; areas declared to be neutral that were not potential targets; and rural areas not likely to be attacked that could receive evacuees. The whole programme was a voluntary one, both for evacuees and those accepting them into their homes. However, the government provided incentives for those willing to accept evacuees. In fact these were inadequate to cover the additional costs and many families providing shelter in this way experienced real hardship. Despite government propaganda, many families were reluctant to participate and when no attacks had occurred by January 1940 during the 'Phoney War', more than a million evacuees returned home. However, in May 1940 when the Germans established bomber bases along the French coast and began to blitz Southampton, Gosport and Portsmouth, another wave of evacuations took place.

The Salvation Army helping an evacuation from Portsmouth and Southampton.

Clearing-up practice in the event of a gas attack.

At first glance it may have seemed a natural reaction on the part of government to seek to get children from vulnerable areas of Hampshire out of harm's way. In practice this meant out of Portsmouth, Southampton and Gosport, although outlying areas of this military/industrial complex such as Eastleigh and the Isle of Wight also suffered the attentions of the Luftwaffe. For the rest it was a case of random bombing with chance serious consequences when buildings were hit such as pubs frequented by military personnel as was the case in Bournemouth. Some families made individual decisions to send their children away or they simply took their chances with their parents. What is striking is the collectivist decisions regarding evacuation made about Hampshire children. Clearly concentration was on the physical reality of moving the children by bus and rail to parts of Hampshire and outside the county considered to be safe. What happened to the children then was largely left to how they were greeted and cared for in places such as Winchester, one of their destinations.

For those organizing the evacuation, the condition of children from the poorer areas of Portsmouth, Southampton and Gosport came as a shock. Dr Victoria Bennett described this as follows: 'There have been complaints in reception areas that children are not only verminous but not even as well trained in home life as a domestic pet.' She went on to say:

> For young children who are dirty in their habits there is some excuse but for bigger children who have brought filthy habits into the homes of clean and decent people there is none. Wallpapers, floor coverings, furniture, bedding and other things have been ruined sometimes beyond repair in the homes of good Samaritans by the dirty ways of the evacuees and the vermin brought with them.

Dr Bennett conceded that the alternative for these children would be to suffer the consequences of saturation bombing. She said, with a perceptible sigh: 'We must train ourselves in the matter of give and take, so that life becomes bearable under these extreme, dangerous, trying conditions.' The Mass Observation Unit reported that households accepting children were appalled both by their physical condition and their behaviour. Many of these children had never tasted fresh food, never slept alone in a bed and never eaten at a table with a knife and fork. In the most extreme cases they had never used a toilet and cases of bed-wetting were not confined to children who were traumatized and unhappy about being separated from their parents. There were problems relating to children suddenly confronted with new diets, or even a countryside ambiance which was summed up in this way: 'Mister, what a lot of blue sky you have here.'

Hampshire County Council recognized the ever-present danger of air-raids. Winchester agreed to take 1,100 children from Portsmouth on the morning of 1 September, beginning with two parties of 400 girls and 150 boys, followed in the afternoon by a further 300 boys. This was organized by Major Pinsent who claimed all the children were safely accommodated in 'good homes'; something not supported by the personal recollections of some of the children. Certainly the organization through Southern Railway and Omnibus was well done. Doreen Bennett describes joining 600 girls at the Girls' Grammar School in Southampton on 2 September with a haversack for clothes, tinned food and a gas mask, all labelled for her evacuation. The gas mask could be fitted to the face via a strap on the side and included a coffee tin attached to a spout containing charcoal to filter out the gas. At Southampton Station she joined thousands of other children, most with no idea of where they were going. Her destination was Bournemouth School for Girls. From there she joined individual parties who walked with their teachers around the streets. She was placed in a household billeting five evacuees comprising Doreen, two friends and two younger sisters. After Dunkirk their school was taken over to billet French soldiers. In Portsmouth the city was divided into seven sectors, each with a dispersal clearance centre. From these assembly points children were moved by bus to Portsmouth Station where special trains were waiting. A further 97,500 children were moved in this way with 66,500 going by rail and 31,000 by bus. Eleven trains departed each day, with checks being made by teaching staff as to eligibility and pamphlets explaining the evacuation issues. For Gosport alone, 3,083 children of school age were evacuated, 784 of pre-school age, 594 mothers accompanied their children, 804 made other evacuation arrangements – often through extended family – and 753 refused to respond. On each train was a marshal supported by staff offering first aid. The exercise employed 110 double-decker buses each day over seven days.

The first train leaving Portsmouth Station in the morning was bound for the Meon Valley, followed by others to Eastleigh and Chandler's Ford. What awaited these children was a whole range of experiences, some positive and some deeply disturbing. Children were introduced to rural life and expected to help in the fields with that summer's harvest.

Evacuation for Betty Reeves from Central School in Portsmouth came on 1 September 1939 and her destination was the Isle of Wight. Betty reported being searched for fleas on arrival at Ryde and carrying brown paper bags with her rations containing corned beef, chocolate and condensed milk. She remembered that it was raining as she and the other children walked in pairs while their teacher knocked on doors seeking a family to take them in. She was finally found somewhere where there were ten sons, nine still in residence. Her mum and dad visited her every Sunday but despite this she remembers crying herself to sleep. For Jean Thorne, evacuated on 2 September 1939, there was the experience of running away from the house where she was billeted in Christchurch which she describes as being like a prison. She and her fellow evacuees ate in the kitchen while the other members of the family dined in the living room. They were set tasks of digging potatoes, creosoting fences, scrubbing and cleaning while the daughters of the family did nothing.

For many Gosport children now embarking on 200 train journeys to Salisbury, Basingstoke, Dunbridge, Winchester, Lyndhurst, Shawford, Eastleigh, Fordingbridge, Stockbridge, Romsey, Swanley and Brockenhurst, the experience represented a leap into the unknown. A total of 12,246 children faced evacuation in this way. For those going to the Isle of Wight the assembly point was Clarence Pier where they were issued with tickets for Ryde. From there it was a train ride to Brading where all disembarked. At Gurnard Holiday Camp where 240 places had been identified, 500 children were packed in. At Chichester the first proposal for evacuation was to put the children under canvas. In some cases the children were treated as servants and were arbitrarily split from their siblings, causing distress. The atmosphere encountered by Jean Thorne made her feel unwelcome as they were treated as dogsbodies. On the other hand, Ronald Lyons' family in Weymouth turned out to be millionaires. Tragically, his father later had to cycle down to inform him that his mother had been killed when the train she was travelling on was bombed.

Perhaps it is the Southampton teacher Eric Wyeth Gadd who gives the best picture of what the events around 1 September were really like. As a teacher he, his wife, and two daughters, Mavis and Wendy, left their house in Southampton to join the general exodus. As well as his luggage, he was carrying his youngest daughter because pushchairs were not allowed. At his school a full check was made that all his party were present with their gas masks, the day's food and approved identification labels. Shepherding the children on to buses to the station yard was watched by 'sad-eyed parents' from the opposite side of the road. His destination was New Milton which was approached through the leafy glades of the New Forest. Awaiting them were their new homes arranged through work by the WVS. He and his colleagues watched as the children were taken to their billets in twos and threes with Gadd wondering where he would sleep that night. His wife reappeared with the good news that their billet could accommodate him as well, together with the news that Warsaw had been bombed and war was now coming.

These evacuees were the lucky ones, being able to take advantage of the late summer weather and bathe at nearby Barton-on-Sea. Advantage was taken of teaching through experience by taking the children into the New Forest to explore the full range of flora and fauna it had to offer. When the fine weather came to an end they were forced to improvise in any building that would provide them with shelter. Gadd reported on the different attitudes of foster parents towards the children. Very few were absolutely devoted to their new charges and they were matched at the other end of the spectrum by families who saw the evacuees as an unbearable nuisance. Between these two points there were the continual difficulties that had to be resolved with the support of the WVS. In October 1940 Gadd was in Lymington Magistrates Court where a gang of youngsters was charged with stealing eggs. By the beginning of 1941 a group of unbilletables had been identified who immediately after arrival from Southampton broke into a chicken coop and devoured its contents. There was heavy drinking involving children as young as 12, as well as an expectation that none of the evacuees should help with the preparation of communal meals provided by volunteers. When work was found for them in nearby Lymington it was refused as being unsuitable. When a foster mother complained of a boy's behaviour, his father in Southampton suggested that Gadd administer severe corporal punishment. As late as August 1941, despite some evacuees returning home Gadd reported that many children remained in their original billet and were well assimilated into their new homes. He noted that 60 per cent of the children had joined the Scouts and Girl Guides. Further, he advanced the case that the children's education had benefited from the evacuation through the enrichment provided by learning in a rural environment. With regard to his school at Ashley, he noted that his children, despite the disruptions, were evenly spread over four levels of attainment.

Gadd believed that in his experience evacuation had not led to deterioration in the behaviour of the children and that where there were problems, these had existed in Southampton prior to evacuation. He cited cases where improvements in behaviour had been observed. The attitude of households where the evacuees were billeted was initially one of suspicion and hostility. This softened as time passed and the children were regarded as a normal part of the life of the district. As the air-raids began in 1940, a distinction was made between the evacuees and the refugees from the blitz.

There were also refugees arriving in Hampshire from Germany. Ursula Kantorowitz arrived with the *kinder* transport. She had been separated from her mother in Hamburg in February 1939 aged just 3. She was met by her uncle in Southampton after a journey from Hamburg. On the Isle of Wight preparations for the arrival of 8,000 evacuated children were made following the declaration of war but only 4,000 arrived.

The Salvation Army seeing off evacuated children.

All aboard: some mothers were going too.

CHAPTER FIVE

The 'Phoney War': Not Phoney for Some

American commentators referred to the stand-off between Germany and Britain and France covering the period from September 1939 to May 1940 as the 'Phoney War'. There were no full-frontal attacks across the German/French border or the air attacks that had been anticipated. In Aldershot important elements of what was to become the British Expeditionary Force (BEF) were assembled prior to moving to France. This consisted of the Coldstream Guards, the Scots Guards, the Royal Warwickshires, the Cheshires, the Borderers, the Second Hampshires, the Dorsets, the Loyal North Lancashires, the Manchesters, the North Staffordshires and the Gordon Highlanders.

The Hampshire battalions received mobilization orders on 25 August when many recruits joined up, not realizing the imminent outbreak of war. Officers received a telegram of mobilization and other ranks a postcard. In Christchurch D Company, 119 soldiers reported on the first day and 120 the next day. Private Giles, a traveller, asked for seventy-two hours to find a home for his donkey. When the declaration of war was announced the battalion sprang into action in the Portsmouth area with companies at Tipner in Portsmouth, Gosport and on the Isle of Wight. Only a small amount of equipment was available to support the training taking place and a considerable amount of imagination had to be employed to make the training realistic. In October, among the sixty new recruits received was the Brighton and Hove footballer Freddie Wilson. Their tasks included the guarding of vulnerable points such as naval armaments depots on the outskirts of Gosport, the ammunition factory at Hardway, Gosport and the munitions depot at Tipner. On the Isle of Wight D Company guarded the boat-builders and the flying boat factory at Cowes. One of their platoons was tasked with guarding the radar station above Ventnor and living in huts. C Company in Fareham was accommodated in a former ammunition dump called The Arches. Following initial enthusiasm for this sort of guard duty, there was a realization of the boredom brought about by the related inactivity. Vic Dent was conscripted twelve days after war broke out, reporting to Lower Barracks, Winchester. He was from Basingstoke and had worked at Thorneycroft's car manufacturing plant.

The second battalion of the Hampshires disembarked at Cherbourg and joined the Gort Line on the Franco/Belgian border. On 14 May 1940 they were moved to the Maginot Line. After the retreat from Dunkirk they were part of home defence. From 1937 there had been frantic efforts to motorize the army and they were instructed to assist the RAF with civil defence. Tim Childerhouse reported thousands of reservists pouring into Aldershot to occupy the barracks of the regular army.

Southampton had always been the major point of departure for British troops going abroad. The Southampton Docks were the last part of England seen by the ill-fated British Expeditionary Force in September and October of 1939. Economic activity in Southampton had benefited from the rush to rearm. Working at Avery, the scales manufacturer, Mrs Drew described the atmosphere in the heady first days of the war. 'Us girls in the office would look out the window and see the poor lads marching down to the docks from their camps along The Avenue,' she remembered. 'They were singing *We're Going to Hang out the Washing on the Siegfried Line*.' Barrage balloons appeared in the sky and at night the phrase 'Put that light out' provided a background commentary from the wardens. Public buildings were reinforced against bomb-blast with sandbags and attempts were made to strengthen windows with sticky paper. Anderson shelters 4ft deep covered with corrugated steel were being assembled in suburban gardens. The population was ordered to carry their gas masks at all times, including the cumbersome ones designed for babies and invalids.

Pamela Lee (née Heath) was 5 years old when war was declared and living in Winton, a suburb of Bournemouth, and she spoke about the darkness and the silence in her household that accompanied the declaration of war. 'Our father came into the room and told us this mysterious concept of war was about to happen but it meant little to us. My mother was required to sign on for war work but was immediately signed off again because she had 3 young children.' Her father's work in a local factory was accepted as a 'reserved occupation' but at night he worked in one of the observation units on the Bournemouth coastline.

There was a realization that Southampton, not only with its aircraft manufacture but its role as a communications hub, would be a prime target for the Germans. To the north at Eastleigh the town was not only a vital railway centre but also a focus for war-related manufacturing activity. Here railway wagons were built and repaired alongside motor boats. RAF rescue boats that would come to play an important role in the Channel were being made at Vosper Thorneycroft, while additional manufacture of other boats took place at British Power Boats based at Hythe on Southampton Water. Alongside the River Itchen submarines were under construction. Following manufacture at Supermarine, the new Spitfire was being tested at Eastleigh aerodrome. HMS *Raven*, the Fleet Air Arm Base training centre, had to accommodate the

Ford motor works. Most important for Britain's later survival was the aviation activity around Hamble Aerodrome with Cunliffe Owen Ltd developing the skills to repair planes enabling them to return to the fray. Clustered together, these factories complemented each other with firms such as Folland Aircraft Ltd and Fairey Aviation working under contract to Supermarine.

As far as possible it was vital that these factories were well camouflaged, not only to protect their industry but also the growing number of women now working in them as men were enlisted into the services.

Rodney Whale was at his grandparents' house in Romsey on the Sunday when war was declared and recalls all their extended family's deep concern about the future. His father was a member of the auxiliary fire service throughout the war. He recalls an American soldier who his father had met in the First World War offering to evacuate him to Kansas. The offer was declined in favour of evacuation to Romsey. Mrs E. Rose recalls her mother crying when she heard Chamberlain's broadcast and the onset of rationing depriving her of Tizer and peanuts. It was 22 December 1939 when troops to be billeted in the small farming community arrived, bringing a different element to Alton's current ARP restrictions. They were joined by Australian soldiers.

Air Commander Felicity Hill recalled joining the 1,734-strong Women's Auxiliary Air Force (WAAF) at Farnborough Aerodrome in 1939 as an equipment assistant where she was regarded as a 'la-de-da female' and allocated menial jobs. Then she failed her officer's board in 1940 because at 23 she was regarded as being 'too young'. Pauline Miles, whose father was a dentist, lived in the centre of Southampton in a prosperous middle-class family. 'Nothing happened for several weeks after the war broke out,' she recalled, 'then long columns of troops were on the move everywhere in Southampton.'

Meanwhile in Canada 50,000 men had volunteered for service in Europe. On 10 December 1939 the first group left Halifax in Canada for Britain and was greeted in Glasgow by an enthusiastic crowd. Twenty-four hours later they arrived in Aldershot as the coldest winter since 1894 was tightening its grip. The Canadians were to occupy the barracks vacated by the Expeditionary Force. Awaiting them were the Wellington Lines, Stanhope Lines and Marlborough Lines which they occupied. They were immediately confronted with shortages illustrated by private cars having to be used to tow guns for exercises. By February 1940 there were 23,304 Canadian soldiers in Aldershot, making preparations for France. In an attempt to bolster the retreating BEF they were sent to Dover, but the situation was becoming so desperate with the BEF in total retreat that the army was forced to change its plans.

No bombs were dropped on the Isle of Wight in 1939, producing a false sense of calm.

Fleet football team, all engaged in the war.

Aldershot's trainee pilots in Canada.

Instruction in gunnery.

CHAPTER SIX

Dunkirk: Britain Stands Alone

The effort to rescue the BEF from the beaches of Dunkirk and the order by Admiral Sir William James to press every available boat into service meant that Portsmouth Harbour was cleared of every vessel. On 29 May 1940 they set sail, comprising minesweepers, destroyers, motor torpedo boats, Hayling Island ferries, Pickfords' fleet of small coasters, trawlers, motor fishing vessels, private yachts, harbour defence vessels, the Solent passenger steamer and even Admiral James's own barge.

The Southern Railways' fleet of paddle-steamers – *Freshwater*, *Sussex Queen*, *Portsdown*, *Sandown* and *Whippington* – crossed to Dunkirk and played a part in rescuing thousands of troops. When the message came that small craft were needed to cross the Channel to rescue thousands of men of the BEF besieged in Dunkirk, paddle-steamers operating along the southern coast sailed out into the Channel to answer the call. Paddle-steamers were operating out of Bournemouth, Southampton and Portsmouth and one of these was called the *Gracie Fields*. It had been launched in Southampton in 1936 by Gracie herself, but she forgot to give the ship a name and belatedly shouted: '*Gracie Fields* goes to sea.' The crowd then all joined in with *Sing As We Go*, a well-known song from the Gracie Fields film of the same name. The *Gracie Fields* joined the armada of ships evacuating Dunkirk and made one crossing successfully. However, on the second trip she was hit by a bomb and badly damaged. Her crew was taken off and HMS *Pangbourne* attempted to tow her back to harbour. Unfortunately she sank because her rudder had been damaged and she was taking on water. Another of the ferries, the *Princess Helena*, survived the evacuation and the *Lorna Doone* worked as a minesweeper. Unfortunately not every mine was located. SS *Portsdown* – operated by Southern Railways and running between Portsmouth and the Isle of Wight – hit a mine on 20 September 1941 and sank off Southsea Beach killing eight members of its crew and an unknown number of passengers.

Although unsuitable for the task of defending the BEF at Dunkirk, planes from Lee-on-Solent were sent to the skies above the besieged British army. With aircraft grossly inferior to those of the Germans it was a suicidal task to try to provide protection from German aerial attack. Two of the aircraft sent were Skuas and Rocs which were mainly used for towing targets during training exercises. Neither of these aircraft possessed a forward-firing gun. If they escaped at all, the planes arrived back in a badly damaged condition.

However, as far as the troops on the ground were concerned, any plane diverting the attacking German planes above them was carrying out an invaluable task.

Tom Burns was called up on 18 January 1940 at the age of 20 for the Highland Light Infantry, although he had stipulated 'Anything but the infantry.' In June 1940 he was transferred from Yeovil to Tidworth Park in Hampshire. Although these were the last desperate days of Dunkirk, his regiment was sent to Cherbourg in the 157th Brigade which included the King's Own Borderers, the Cameronians and the 5th Battalion, Highland Light Infantry. They were in trenches facing a German advance about 20 miles from Paris. Burns told of trying to use mortars for which they had never received training and just stopping his mate from putting a primed shell into the mortar the wrong way round, which would have blown up the pair of them. A German mortar landed just a few yards from them, which fortunately was a dud. The company commander then issued the instruction 'Every man for himself', meaning that they had to get back to Cherbourg in whatever way they could. One of his friends who spoke fluent French suggested that he stay and take his chances in France. However, Burns decided to stay with the bulk of the army. In Cherbourg they encountered the hostility of the townspeople who accused them of desertion. On the boat to Southampton they were dive-bombed by Stukas. They were anchored in the Solent with a rumour that they were going to be posted to the Middle East, which caused great concern after their experiences in France. He described landing in Southampton, filthy with fleas, lice and dirt. During his current affairs lectures in Southampton it emerged that the 157th had been sent as a gesture to the French people when all was lost in France. They were regarded as sacrificial lambs that were never expected to come back again.

Joan Davis in Calshot remembered seeing exhausted men from Dunkirk on boats in Southampton Water. Some of them were half-naked. Clothing was collected for the filthy, lousy evacuees who had lost all their possessions. She described the terrible stench that surrounded them and how she thought 'the real war begins here.' As well as this there was a shortage of regular soldiers to defend the naval installations in the event of an invasion. Volunteers were hastily recruited to man the perimeters of these bases armed with weapons described as 'museum pieces', or in the case of the dockyards Lee Enfield rifles from the Great War. From the outset in Portsmouth real communication problems existed between civil defence and emergency services. The code word adopted was 'Cromwell' which was in operation on 26 May 1940 when the moon and tide appeared to be conspiring to produce an ideal date for a German invasion.

Bournemouth was experiencing problems with its siren system based on the Town Hall when a test the day before war was declared saw the sound being carried away by the wind. The complete blackout had resulted in an increase in road accidents in the borough and nearby rural areas. However, an auxiliary fire service had come into existence and water tanks mounted on buses also appeared. Gas masks had been distributed to everyone on 16 December 1939, despite claims of apathy due to the difficulty of recruiting wardens.

Because of the Isle of Wight's proximity to the French coast it was natural that it would play an important part in the evacuation fleet. These vessels were either conscripted or went voluntarily. Would the Germans follow the evacuation fleet? There was some comfort for the islanders with the arrival of the 6th Black Watch in June but morale was weakened by the revelation that a plane shot down on 23 June had been British. By 14 June bombs were falling on the Isle of Wight.

On 8 June 1940 the king arrived in Aldershot to inspect the Canadians and New Zealanders who had been diverted from their intended destination of Egypt to provide defence in Hampshire. On 6 July at 4.15 pm nine HE bombs fell on Guillemont Barracks in Knollys Road, killing three and injuring thirty. On 2 and 16 August the nearby RAE at Farnborough was hit by twenty HE bombs. The environment in which troops were sent to guard the RAE was a bleak one with total blackout and inadequate heating in a bitter winter. However, gradually places of entertainment such as dance halls came into existence featuring band leaders such as Duke Ellington. Five cinemas had now reopened after initially being closed. Saturday night became 'fight night', placing pressure on local police. One, a policeman going about his duty, was thrown through a fish and chip shop window in Cove. The army was looking for ways in which the Canadians could be deployed, such as in the raid on St Nazaire. Perhaps this produced an overconfidence that contributed towards the disastrous raid on Dieppe on 19 August 1942.

On the days following the Dunkirk evacuation, Dutch, Belgian and French airmen arrived in Britain wanting to continue the fight against Germany. In response the RAF No. 1 Training School was formed at Odiham with an inheritance of obsolete fighter and bomber aircraft that had been flown there. General de Gaulle paid a visit shortly after their arrival and a decision was made to disperse the foreign airmen to other squadrons.

The realization of the existentialist threat faced by the country stimulated a level of war production that was to exceed that of Germany. At Wellworthys in Lymington, Rolls Royce-trained engineer Ivor Carlisle from Bolton added his mechanical skills to teams of employees; increasingly female as men were conscripted. These skills were recognized and he travelled throughout Hampshire on his motorbike helping with the manufacture of machine tools. On one occasion on entering one of the many military control zones in late 1940 he failed to hear the order to stop. He showed with pride the hole the guard's bullet had made in his crash helmet. Thelma Ryder, conscripted from Plymouth, spoke of working in her heavy blue overalls as she made piston rings, producing a response from her mother when she sent her a photo saying 'I've never seen you in trousers before.' Thelma described Wellworthys as being a happy factory and doing piece-work required her to produce a certain number of piston rings each day. If her machine operated too fast the operator was likely to get particles of steel in her eye because no protective masks were issued. Twelve hours were worked each day and the pay was £3 per week. However, Ivor Carlisle expressed concern about some of the safety practices of the firm and in 1942 brought the workers there out on strike to improve safety in the Lymington factory.

Pamela Lee described how the threat of invasion became a reality in people's lives. She spoke of a dreadful night when the family was at Mill Farm, 10 miles from Bournemouth. Her mother had been a Land Girl in the Great War and had introduced her to the satisfaction of tasks associated with rural life such as milking. Her mother had woken them early with the news that there had been an invasion on the nearby coastline. Pamela's father and a group from nearby farms had been up all night with pitchforks and obsolete guns. Her mother's instruction was to take the children and drive north away from the coast. Back in Bournemouth after the false alarm, she described seeing French soldiers sitting on the pavements around the houses where they lived. Her father came to have responsibility for a Home Guard platoon and was determined to pass their discipline on to his children. On the instruction of 'gas', his children had to don their gas masks and because he had access to a gas chamber he insisted that his family take part in exercises there as well. A large map was placed on the wall above her rocking horse on which the battles taking place were displayed. She also recalled that when toilet paper became unavailable, the family cut up newspapers which hung on a string in their WC.

Second New Zealand Expeditionary Force in Hampshire in 1940 being inspected by Winston Churchill.

Route marches under the threat of war.

Regional regimental dinner of the Hampshire Regiment based in Kent in 1940.

Mother and son: he was one of the few survivors of HMS Hood *sunk in 1940.*

HMS Hood: *many young men from Hampshire were killed on board in 1940.*

New field gun being presented.

CHAPTER SEVEN

Defending Hampshire:
The Armed Forces

It was logical that the Germans would follow up on the British defeat at Dunkirk and move to invade Britain as soon as possible. In order for an invasion fleet to cross the Channel, the Luftwaffe would have to achieve dominance of the skies and Hampshire's beaches. Because the British navy had dominated the German navy in the exchanges in Norway, only air superiority would prevent a loss of capital ships. (Much of the technical information in this chapter is referenced from *Defending Hampshire* by Mike Osborne which contains many specifications and other important data.)

That the focus of the Battle of Britain for Germany would be in the air was not known in Britain, so land-based preparations under General Ironside, Commander-in-Chief of Home Forces, were set in motion. It was crucial that the Germans should not be allowed to establish themselves on Hampshire beaches and defensive resources were allocated to what he referred to as the 'coastal crust'. Behind this would be a network of anti-tank defences designed to slow down the advance of tanks inland. After Dunkirk Ironside had almost no tanks, mobile artillery or transport, so delay on the beaches for the invaders was essential. In this he was reliant on the navy to prevent the reinforcement of any beachhead established by the Germans. Aldershot, Southampton and Portsmouth were to become fortress towns having their own defensive perimeter.

Of necessity, defences in the Solent would be crucial to protect Portsmouth and Southampton. The Needles and Spithead were protected with 9.2in guns, two at New Needles Battery on the west and two more each at Culver Down and Nodes Point to the east. Only at Southsea Castle were there two 9.2in guns defending the eastern approach located on the mainland. The role of 6in guns was the prevention of warships getting in close to the shore to assist landing barges with new batteries at Bouldnor and Cliff End at the western end and Nodes Point and Yaverland on the east. All of these had two guns each. Spithead had forts at Horse Sand and No Man's Land with pairs of guns. Spitbank had a single gun. Mountings were improved to give the guns greater range so that they could provide greater coverage of coastal waters. Guns were also mounted to cover the narrower channels as a measure

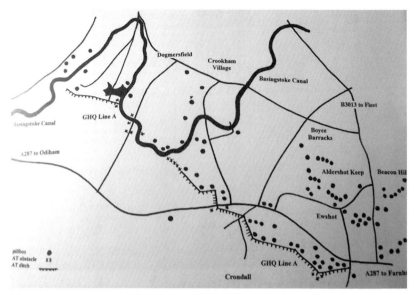

The defensive line around Aldershot (from Defending Hampshire).

against motorboats attacking moored vessels. There was a twin 6-pounder with a range of 3 miles and a traverse of 360 degrees. It was capable of firing forty rounds per minute from each of its barrels. They were deployed in the bottlenecks of the Solent such as Hurst Castle, Fort Albert in the Needles Passage, Fort Blockhouse and Point Battery in Portsmouth Harbour. There were two 12-pounder quick-firing (QF) guns guarding Southampton Water, Calshot Castle employing crossed fire with Bungalow Battery on the eastern bank. There was a need for specialist manpower to operate these increasingly specialist guns, plus a need to camouflage the guns against dive-bombers; concrete covered by camouflage materials was employed for this purpose.

Guns were even sited to attack Portsmouth in the event of it being captured by the Germans. They were deployed to cover areas between Portsmouth, Portland and Newhaven. The greater part of Hampshire's coastline was covered by guns running from Sandbanks in Poole Harbour. Batteries were installed at Southbourne in April 1941 and at Mudeford in May 1941.

On the beaches any gun that could be found after Dunkirk was fixed into a gunhouse, fieldworks, a pit with sandbags or any similar construction. Heavy naval guns were placed at Hurst Castle together with other lighter guns. Along the Hampshire coasts these lighter guns were installed at suitable points. As far as mobile guns were concerned, the 3rd Infantry Division associated with Hampshire and the Isle of Wight was given the role and for Portsmouth the 119th Field Regiment attached to Portsmouth's 50th Division employed howitzers dating from the Great War. Only twenty-five 4in guns originally made at the Portsmouth dockyard proved to be available. Much heavy artillery had been lost in France and there was difficulty in obtaining replacements. Experiments were conducted to set light to flammable fuel on the Solent and at Moody's Down near Sutton Scotney. Work to develop incendiary vessels against landing craft also took place. Obstacles were put in place at Sowley near Lepe to impede the operation of landing craft, together with poles to prevent amphibious aircraft landing on beaches.

A whole range of pill-boxes came under consideration by the War Office, usually featuring shellproof structures and a Vickers machine gun with construction that would prevent attack from the rear. At Ringwood a line was created capable of accommodating ten men with a Bren gun and rifles, while at Everton reliance was placed on a converted building. Breamore Mill had twenty-six pill-boxes and at Lymington and Beaulieu ad hoc structures were built. Ditches were dug linking pill-boxes and other structures together. Roads were blocked by obstacles and barbed wire was laid to inhibit movement. Mines and pits were dug, providing a defending infantry with greater flexibility.

Britain's main line of defence entered Hampshire a mile east of Riseley where the Blackwater and Whitewater rivers meet within the boundaries of the Aldershot Command. The line followed the Whitewater to the Basingstoke Canal and along the canal to Crookham village and Ewshot. The Aldershot Command placed strong emphasis on defence in depth with forward positions such as Odiham. A defensive spine was created through a continuous string of pill-boxes. Where the Basingstoke Canal parts company from the GHQ defensive line west of Hancock's Farm, defensive positions were reinforced for 10 miles with artificial anti-tank ditches. At Crookham Wharf and the village, three shellproof pill-boxes were created. Steps were taken to prevent the passage of tanks across the canal. Aldershot identified the need for twenty-one platoon-sized companies to hold these installations along the GHQ Defence Line A. The role fell to the Oxford and Buckinghamshire Light Infantry and the newly-arrived troops from Canada and New Zealand. Artillery regiments with 13- and 18-pounder field guns were further bolstered by new equipment and three infantry brigades. A formidable barrier had been created. At Fleet, for instance, there were fifteen bulletproof and shellproof pill-boxes and four Stent (prefabricated) pillboxes, together with two pairs of Vickers machine-gun emplacements. There were no permanent garrisons but the concept of their usage was that they would spring into action should an invasion take place. Planning for Aldershot defence involved a mixture of infantry battalions, Royal Engineer battalions from Longmoor Camp and Canadian and New Zealand troops. In an area defending the army's principal base, a large proportion of the guns being used were obsolete. The sector between Dogmersfield Lake and Culverlands east of Farnham operating 20-, 13- and 18-pounder guns from the Great War manned by the 2nd New Zealand Division, who had only four relatively modern 2-pounder guns.

Various points along the lines drawn up for defence were identified as places where tanks could be resisted and delayed. Initially Portsmouth, Southampton and Romsey were identified to perform this function. In September eighteen anti-tank islands were identified including places such as Christchurch, Ringwood, Fordingbridge, Dunbridge, Totton, Andover and Basingstoke. The vital strategic area between Southampton and Portsmouth, Bishop's Waltham and Botley, had anti-tank provision. Alton, Liphook, Liss and Odiham were regarded as key points forward of the GHQ line. Of A tank island status were Portsmouth, Winchester, Christchurch and Totton; Botley, Ringwood and Bursledon were B status; while Basingstoke, Andover and Beaulieu were given C status, indicating the priority given to each location. The idea was to suck any attack into a battle that would diminish the momentum of the advancing enemy and threaten their supply chain. Following its formation, the Home Guard manned posts at Buriton and Privett railway tunnels as well as manning road blocks sealing off Fareham.

Plans were brought into play that turned the hundreds of miles covered by the Aldershot Command into an armed camp. The process turned the area into a large fortress. In 1941 the Germans' use of paratroopers during the battle for Crete raised the prospect of a similar attack on Aldershot. Both Farnborough with its Royal Aircraft Establishment (RAE) and Aldershot with its vast barracks were seen as inviting an attack of this kind. Strategic lines for defence in Aldershot itself ran from Basingstoke Canal through the centre of the town and back to the canal employing barriers between the barrack buildings and obstacles to airborne attack. However, this unfortunately failed to offer any defence against the enemy's strategic objectives. The commander of the garrison, in the absence of effective guns, put in an urgent request for a newly-developed mortar. Fortunately the storemen, drivers, mechanics and non-combatants who occupied Aldershot were not required to defend it with the 6,000 rifles seen to be available. Even after the German invasion of the Soviet Union, neither anti-tank (AT) guns nor armour were available for the defence of Aldershot.

Both Portsmouth and Southampton possessed garrisons capable of defending their perimeter. There was defence around coastal artillery batteries at Whale Island: the shore-based HMS *Excellent* with two 12- and two 6-pound guns manned by a mixture of Royal Navy and Home Guard personnel. Towns were given tanks after the Great War but most had been scrapped by the mid-1930s except the one at Southsea which was adapted to become a mobile pill-box adjacent to a bridge on Whale Island. At Portsea Island a spigot mortar was installed, together with a circular pill-box and a 75mm gun in a concrete gunhouse. This was manned by 200 seamen from HMS *Anson* acting as a defence group while their ship was being refitted.

There was a realization that defence required an almost continuous AT barrier plus an anti-submarine boom after the sinking of the *Ark Royal* in Scapa Flow by a submarine that had penetrated shallow water. Concrete machine-gun emplacements were built at Eastney Forts East and West and some were placed inland along the eastern shore, with a cluster of pill-boxes at Hilsea Halt. The shoreline between Paulsgrove and Portchester was given AT blocks plus a number of pill-boxes. Dockyard companies such as Airspeed and Vospers received protection in the form of the 29th and 32nd battalions with the 31st Battalion going to Cosham and the General Post Office Battalion to Southsea. If the situation had become desperate, depot staff, naval instructors and training ratings could have been called upon, while a battalion of young seamen from HMS *Excellent* armed only with rifles and twenty rounds of ammunition could be deployed against an attack on Gosport Peninsula.

Southampton's protection against marine raids relied on QF guns at the mouth of Southampton Water together with barrage balloon vessels HMS *Carmenita* and *Polita* providing defence from 1939. Road blocks and AT placement sought to guard against attacks from other directions. Three battalions of the Hampshire Territorials guarded Southampton Docks and other troops were deployed throughout the county. The Scottish 52nd (Lowland) Division was at Andover, while the 4th Infantry Division was in Portsmouth. In October 1940 the 38th Welsh Infantry Division moved to Aldershot, coinciding with the arrival of the Canadian Corps.

In January 1940 the Hampshire Battalion moved to Marston House near Frome. In a particularly severe winter for some it was accommodation in tents in the grounds of Marston House. Even those accommodated in cottages on the estate had to draw icy water from a stream in order to wash and shave. In the large mansion all heat, light and water had been turned off. Training involved saluting all officers but one new recruit on guard duty, leaping to attention in response to the arrival of an officer, forgot that he had a fixed bayonet which then fixed itself to the roof of his sentry box!

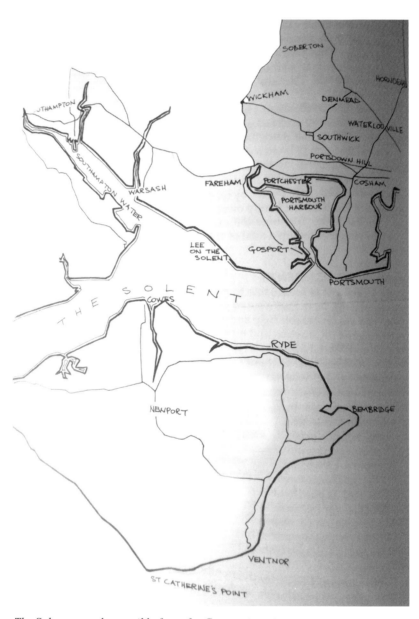

The Solent area, the possible focus for German invasion.

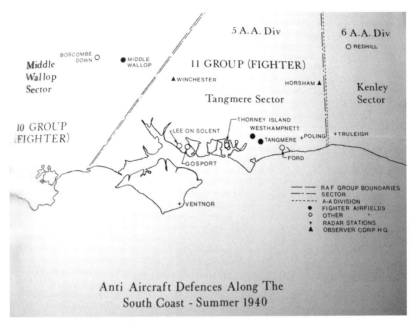

Anti-aircraft defence in Hampshire.

Beechleigh Home Guard with its commander who may have been the prototype for the Dad's Army *sitcom's Captain Mainwaring.*

Home Guard unit, Lymington.

East Meon Home Guard unit.

King George VI inspecting troops in Aldershot.

Members of the Canadian Corps recently arrived in Britain.

CHAPTER EIGHT

Defending Hampshire: The Civilian Dimension

Throughout Hampshire moves were made to prepare for invasion, either by sea or air. Analysis suggested that the main threat would come from an invasion force landing on the south coast exploiting the valley of the Avon. There was desperate urgency to create stop lines in the form of pill-boxes, anti-tank emplacements and the training of an underground army. Initially what came to be known as the Home Guard was referred to as the Local Defence Volunteers (LDV). On 14 May 1940 Anthony Eden, Secretary of State for War, appealed for men between the ages of 17 and 65 to come forward in defence of the country. In the end boys aged just 14 and elderly men of 80 joined. As long as those presenting themselves were fit they were usually recruited. Within twenty-four hours 250,000 had joined nationwide and by the end of May 1940 this had risen to 400,000, reaching a peak in September 1943 of 1.7 million.

One in four of the Home Guard were veterans of the Great War, meaning that initially their average age was high. Later the over-65s were retired and there was an influx of teenagers, resulting in 1943 in only one in fourteen being an ex-serviceman and the average age was 30. Home Guard officers were often dignitaries in the community and leaders in lower ranks in recognition of their local knowledge, experience and status.

At first organizationally no one was quite sure how the Home Guard would operate but a clearer view of this emerged from July following a broadcast by Churchill referring to them as the Home Guard. Following Dunkirk, weapons were scarce, even in the army. It was a case of finding what weapons existed within the community. It appeared that the most powerful weapon was the Molotov cocktail (a type of petrol bomb). Later Thompson machine guns, Sten guns and Bren guns were made available and with training by qualified instructors the Home Guard became an efficient force wearing uniforms with LDV on the back. Proper uniforms only appeared belatedly.

In May 1940 there was a universal fear that invasion would come very shortly and this general acceptance resulted in an effective relationship between the Home Guard and the civil defence services, meaning that Home Guard personnel received training in dealing with the aftermath of air-raids and, vice versa, air-raid wardens were trained in the duties of the Home Guard. When the blitz began, Home Guard personnel distinguished themselves in rescue work. Fortunately no gas attacks occurred but Home Guard units were well versed in methods of decontamination. A Home Guard battalion usually consisted of 11,000 members that were divided into companies usually numbering four. Hampshire battalions included the 3rd Hampshire based in Basingstoke, 4th Hampshire based in Aylesford, 24th Hampshire based in Alton and 27th Hampshire based in Farnborough.

Many of those in the Home Guard were in reserved jobs which prevented them from enlisting or being conscripted. They came from the Portsmouth dockyard, Southampton docks or worked in the aircraft factories of Hamble, Portsmouth and Woolston. Some of the battalions were directly tied to particular trades such as the General Post Office Battalion, the Southern Railway Battalion and the Portsmouth Electricity Undertaking. Rural areas based their battalion on the nearest town or city but kept smaller units of organization around their own village and they could be asked to man the defence of that village. The 27th Farnborough Battalion had the responsibility of guarding the Royal Military Academy, manning one of the War Office's fixed defensive positions and a general responsibility for defending Aldershot to the last man. Encouragement was given to the Home Guard to develop their own strategy for the defence of their immediate area. For example, Beaulieu was defended through four reinforced points. These were Mill Yard, Mill House Dairy and the Mangold House behind the Clock House. The original concept of the Home Guard was defensive but as the war continued it was allowed to adopt a proactive role which involved mounting patrols into areas where patrols relying on vehicles found difficulty in monitoring. General Montgomery himself made time to visit some of the smallest Home Guard village units. Even when small arms became available, genuine difficulties were experienced in obtaining artillery. However, as with Aldershot where regular soldiers were equipped with spigot mortars, 4,000 of these were made available for the defence of airfields and the Home Guard elsewhere.

At Christchurch the holder of the world speed record, Sir Malcolm Campbell, mounted a Hotchkiss QF gun on a truck; an early form of a self-propelled gun. Due to concern about the number of accidents that had occurred when Home Guard units experimented with weapons, an instruction was given to use only approved weaponry. By 1941 the Home Guard had turned itself into a well-managed and well-equipped part of the defensive structure of the country. The reality of *Dad's Army* with which we are all familiar was elderly farmers, doctors and drivers, and Captain Mainwaring who may have been Lieutenant Colonel Crofton with a determination to fight to the last man in Beaulieu. Given no chance against the invading German panzers, Crofton had drawn up detailed maps of how the Germans could be delayed long enough for the regular army to counter-attack. Part of their task involved defending Fawley Oil Refinery with fuel lines and road links through the New Forest.

The initial thinking about defence involved trenches and pill-boxes, an analysis that had to rapidly be altered with the advent of paratroopers and the rapid advances enabled by airborne attacks. In Gosport the call was received to form a Home Guard unit and the expectation was that just twenty-five men would come forward. In reality hundreds of men besieged Gosport Police Station to enlist. In the end Gosport boasted a platoon of 450 men. By 1 September 1942 Gosport Home Guard Battalion, part of the Hampshire Regiment, comprised 1,250 men. Hundreds of men carried out night duties while maintaining their occupations working as guards or lookouts, in laying piquets or as beach patrols. Dora Piper talks of the younger members of the Home Guard digging defensive positions at strongpoints on roads around the Denmead area, providing delays or destruction of enemy transport. Stocks of Molotov cocktails were made ready, together with 45-gallon tar barrels ready to be rolled onto the road being built up along with mines and booby traps. Farm workers in the area had to juggle their Home Guard activities with work in the fields, adding to their sixty hours of this work with twenty hours of patrolling, drilling and range-firing during the hot summer months of 1940. This Home Guard group was adequately armed, having Lewis and Thompson machine guns. Where the military considered it necessary, road blocks were established with flying patrols, although in some cases these were set up without instruction. These patrols ran into difficulty with senior officers who disputed their authority to check them at these points. They were also charged with monitoring fifth column activities. At Bishop's Waltham, Ron Cook was excused guard duty because he was involved in restoring power supplies for West Hampshire Electricity following raids. These men were supplied with Canadian Ross .303 rifles and ten rounds of ammunition. The remains of a platoon of Royal Engineers from Dunkirk in possession of two lorries formed part of Cook's group. Pipe grenades of 1in diameter were constructed, filled with gelignite and designed to be lit with a slow match.

At Sway in the New Forest a casualty service was organized through the Home Guard with a local doctor and his staff linked into civil defence. All street signs were removed to disorientate any invader. Desmond Hollie describes how he and his 7- and 8-year-old friends would use their bows and arrows against the Germans. They made many arrows, coating them with cow dung, and secreted them in caches in the forest ready for an ambush by the Nazi soldiers. At the time this was their deadly purpose. At Boldre in the New Forest Gerald Duplessis raised the local Home Guard. He had the rank of captain as a former member of the Hampshire Territorial Battalion in the First World War. The Boldre group was divided into four sections: Boldre and Sandy Down, Pilley and Bull Hill, Walhampton and Portmore, and Baddesley and Norley. Half of the men had been in Duplessis' company in the Great

War. He collected them as a result of a tour through local villages. The Boldre section was led by a retired parson and contained two retired majors and an admiral, while Walhampton had a brigadier and three colonels just as volunteers. One of the sections in the area even boasted a field marshal.

Headquarters was in Duplessis' house with the drawing room doubling up as the store room. The platoon's transport was a Baby Austin which carried greatcoats and boxes of ammunition together with a cocker spaniel. No uniforms were available apart from an LDV armband. However, by the autumn of 1940 they were issued with shapeless denim uniforms. The local school platoon eventually had Officers' Training Corps (OTC) rifles, some of which worked, but for the village Local Defence Group weapons consisted of whatever could be dredged up. For them the first weapons to come in the autumn were Browning automatic rifles and Thompson machine guns. These were strictly rationed to one per platoon. In working out tactics there was no evidence of the guerrilla warfare that had been previously employed against the British Empire across the world. Tom Driberg, who had some experience of the Spanish Civil War, was one of the authors of the Home Guard's handbook but the main thrust of its content related to trench warfare in France. Defence was to be of a static nature with an expectation that attacking tanks could be stopped by volunteers in sandbagged trenches. As the war progressed there was a realization of the danger of invasion led by parachutists and the Home Guard was given the role of watching for them. In the exercises carried out with the Northampton Fusiliers on Sunday mornings, the volunteers' enthusiasm declined markedly after 12.30 pm when the Wagon and Horses inn opened its doors. Using a sandpit at the firing range at Brockenhurst, some of the volunteers found it difficult to even hit the sandpit. It should be appreciated that because of their proximity to the coast, these men were effectively in the front line. However, the only shot fired throughout the war was by an Etonian schoolboy who accidentally fired his rifle.

As well as the official Home Guard organization, secret groups called auxiliary units were set up. They were put together as a result of a trawl of gamekeepers, poachers and boy scouts tasked to sabotage the enemy once they were in occupation of the country. In Hampshire they established occupational bases in which they lurked, waiting until the invaders had moved on. There were thirteen such groups in Hampshire commanded by Captain Clive operating through hidden wireless communication. If nothing else, the skills learned in the organization proved invaluable to its younger recruits who joined the commandos. At the time of D-Day, when the threat of invasion had receded, members of this auxiliary group were sent via Portsmouth to the Isle of Wight in case the Germans mounted a counter-attack there and in the Solent. After two weeks when nothing had happened, they were returned to their bases.

Praise was forthcoming from the *Aldershot News* for a training display given by the town's Home Guard described as 'meretricious'. They paraded behind the headquarters, showing how they had progressed since their formation in 1940; some of them had been armed with shotguns, making a comparison with the tommy guns and contemporary equipment they now possessed. This was followed by displays by the ambulance section, demonstrations of unarmed combat and a demonstration of firing drill. Even if the perceived danger invasion had passed by the end of 1940, the operation of the Home Guard served to militarize communities.

The Home Guard at the RAE was able to build on a high degree of accuracy achieved by members of their rifle club. Its Home Guard featured a high degree of democracy with due recognition being given to members with Great War experience. In the best tradition of *Dad's Army*, a scientist stepped forward and said he wanted to volunteer for a suicide mission. The assembled group were not over-impressed by this gesture because he had proved singularly incompetent in all the military exercises in which he had played a part. A member spoke of the difficulty conveying passwords when a member of the Home Guard unit spoke with a heavy Irish brogue. An incident when a Sten gun was being stripped and reassembled occurred during an inspection. The weapon had a difficult spring that was allowed to engage, resulting in a large part of the gun striking the visitor. In May 1944 the RAE Home Guard went to Seaford in Sussex on exercises and was able to observe a pre D-Day landing in Newhaven harbour.

CHAPTER NINE

The Royal Navy and the Dockyards

As with the vast Aldershot Command, the Portsmouth Command covered an area from Newhaven to Seaton and had a sub-command at Portland and jurisdiction that stretched to the Surrey border. It contained the key elements in the Solent relating to Britain's survival. The command built, maintained, converted and repaired scores of ships. It was here that ships were supplied and sailors trained in new techniques as the war developed. The great task of supporting and supplying the navy was focused in Portsmouth with its dockyard that refitted 2,500 vessels and provided berthing for 2,365 more to enable repairs carried out by 40,000 men and women. From June 1940 they were under constant attack. Although this meant that large-scale vessel construction could not be achieved, twenty new lattice masts for destroyers were completed, together with floating docks for escort vessels. Conversion work was always required, with merchant ships being armed and trawlers becoming minesweepers.

Portsmouth was the location for developmental work in midget submarines, neutralizing magnetic mines, landing craft design, the Mulberry harbour and PLUTO which will be discussed later. As the severity of the air attacks increased, it became necessary to disperse some of the dockyard's work. By 1944 Portsmouth had become the centre for a small fleet containing trawlers with anti-submarine devices, minesweepers and vessels for patrol and boom defence as well as many vessels for harbour defence. In early 1940 HMS *Hornet* was established as a base for defence along the coast. After not being taken seriously at first, construction work at Gosport of motor gun boats (MGBs), motor torpedo boats (MTBs) and motor fishing vessels (MFVs) provided a flotilla enabling HMS *Hornet* to achieve a fine reputation for coastal defence. However, moves to develop combined operations between the navy and the army were undermined by the disastrous raid on Dieppe in August 1942. The army force principally comprised 6,000 Canadians from Bordon in the Aldershot Command who embarked from Southampton and Portsmouth under the jurisdiction of the Portsmouth Command. More than half of them became casualties in what was an ill-managed and ill-conducted venture in conflict with the views of Admiral James, the commander in Portsmouth.

It was apparent that the crucial defence would be against aerial attack on vulnerable military targets in Hampshire. In July 1940 crucial decisions were taken to allocate forty-four guns to Portsmouth, forty-three guns to Southampton and later eight guns to Bramley. Across Hampshire in designated areas assorted machine guns, some of which were mounted, were located and supported by the 35th AA Brigade. An initial decision was made to deploy 3.7in guns because these were cheaper. At vital points AA sites would consist of 200 men housed in a hut. By 1941 such sites had been expanded to cover Fort Fareham, Beaulieu and Winslow, West End, Cosham, Bedhampton and Hayling Island. It was generally considered that the ideal AA weapon was a 40mm Bofors gun developed in Sweden and made under licence in Britain. In the dockyards guns were borrowed from vessels being refitted. At the Vulcan building a 12-pound gun mounted on a 10-ton lorry shot down a German Ju 88 combat aircraft, while the medieval Arundel Tower supported a 40m Bofors and Fort Blockhouse two 40mm Bofors guns. Further AA defence was achieved by mounting guns on ships such as *Ryde*, *Laguna Belle* in Portsmouth and the *Thames Queen* in Southampton. In 1941 work began to develop a system of unrotated rockets consisting of sixty-four projectors mounted in groups of sixteen and usually manned by the Home Guard. Other sites given protection were Basingstoke and Aldershot with four 3.7in heavy anti-aircraft (HAA) guns. As far as barrage balloons were concerned, in 1939 a balloon group based in the Southampton/Portsmouth area operated with 120 balloons. Squadron 924 operated thirty-two balloons at Portsmouth and at Gosport Squadron 933 had twenty-four, the operation being largely run by the Women's Royal Air Force (WRAF).

The most distinctive aspect of the camouflage attempted was that it depended on smoke screens. The army unit producing the smoke received a warning when the attacking planes were 120 miles away and when 80 miles distant they started the machine that produced the smoke. Oil was laid on rivers and harbours to darken them so that they were no longer a beacon and guide for attacking bombers, with the Solent and Southampton being examples of this.

CHAPTER TEN

Hampshire's Battle for Britain

Following Dunkirk, modifications to the Spitfire at the Woolston Southampton works of Supermarine continued. Engineers Joe Smith and Alan Clifton capitalized on the British advantage of 470 fighters to the 178 German single-seater fighters. Despite this, only 15,000 man hours had been devoted to the Spitfire. At Woolston Ted Pickering moved from flying boats to testing Spitfires. He had flown his first Spitfire on 25 March 1936. J. Samuel White started work fabricating the fuselage for 310 Spitfires and 600 Hurricanes. By the end of the war 11,900 Spitfires had been built. In 1939 Supermarine used reclaimed land on the shore of the Solent to continue their work on amphibious aircraft. Unfortunately this all came to a halt on 11 September 1940 when eighty-seven Ju 87 Stukas attacked Supermarine's Eastleigh works. This was followed by an attack on 15 September on Supermarine at Woolston that killed ninety-two people. As a result, in order to keep production of the Spitfire and Hurricane going, work had to be relocated to a wide range of alternative locations around Southampton. These included the Sunlight Laundry, Hendys Garage, Shorts Garage, Chiswells Garage, Austin House Garage and the Hants and Dorset Bus Depot.

At the RAE in Farnborough, Beatrice Shilling had produced a method of overcoming engine failure when the Spitfire created negative gravity in a steep dive through a device that ensured the continued flow of fuel through the carburettor.

In the skies above Hampshire and on its airfields many of the crucial events of the Battle of Britain took place. Middle Wallop was a Fighter Command base with four squadrons and because it was so crowded 238 Squadron had to fly to nearby Chilbolton to provide a base. From September 1940 difficulty was experienced in combating German fighters at night. Based at Middle Wallop, 200 Bristol Blenheim bombers were equipped with four machine guns beneath the fuselage, adding to their gun turret. These were manufactured at Southern Railway's Ashford factory and although the planes had failed in daytime combat, after being fitted with the first airborne radar they were to prove their worth. The planes' radar operated by sending out wireless signals that identified enemy aircraft on a cathode tube inside its cockpit.

Originally Middle Wallop was intended to be a bomber base under Bomber Command and building began in 1935 of barracks for the crews and ground

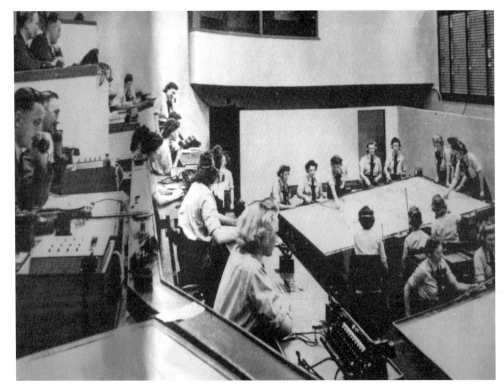

The control room at Middle Wallop airfield base during the Battle of Britain.

crews necessary for bombers. Five large hangars were built and a bomb storage site away from the airfield. The bitter winter of 1939/40 seriously delayed construction with the handover not taking place till April 1940. Conditions during this period were primitive, including a shortage of drinking water. The base had taken on the role of a major training centre which dramatically changed when Fighter Command recognized Middle Wallop's potential as a base for fighter aircraft. A fighter group was assembled, commanded by Vice Marshal Sir Quinton Brand, and Middle Wallop was designated Sector Y. An additional building for the group to operate was constructed. During this period 601 Squadron, battle-scarred from the skies above Dunkirk, flew into the base. The airfield boasted a huge spotlight as part of its defence and small-arms issues against the event of a parachute attack.

Three fighter squadrons were now based at Middle Wallop. No. 238 that brought Spitfires with them from Tangmere on 20 June 1940, 609 Squadron from the West Riding on 5 July 1940 as well as Blenheims also assembled at the base. In the heat of the battle some of 609's aircraft flew to a satellite base at Warmwell, remaining there till dusk before returning to Middle Wallop.

No. 609 Squadron, an auxiliary unit, consisted of volunteers from brewing, farming and milling in Yorkshire. Paul Beaver, a military expert, says of 609 Squadron: 'They were a very successful unit based around their esprit de corps. In August they came into their own.'

In the meantime 238 Squadron exchanged their Spitfires for Hurricanes and sought to develop night-flying combat skills. On 8 August at 9.00 am a convoy named 'Peewit' sailed from the Thames Estuary with twenty ships and was immediately attacked by Stukas operating out of St Malo and Lannion. The convoy was carrying 40,000 tons of coal and coke for industry in the south of England. There should have been four destroyers defending the convoy but in fact there were only two. The attack on the convoy recommenced at 12.45 pm, this time with fifty-seven Stukas escorted by Me 109s of the JG (*Jagdgeschwader*) 27, resulting in major damage to many of the ships. Four merchant vessels were sunk and the rest limped around the Isle of Wight where they were attacked again despite Squadrons 43, 145 and 152 shooting down three Stukas and damaging another four. Squadrons 238 and 609 had been involved in the convoy's defence, shooting down two Me 110s and an Me 109 with a possible four further kills with a loss of three of their own. Two of the squadrons' airmen were lost and a third rescued from the sea by HMS *Bassett* and taken to Haslar Hospital in Gosport.

Middle Wallop squadrons were called upon again to defend the two convoys 'Arena' and 'Agent', attacked as they left the Thames Estuary, while 'Snail' and 'Cable' departing Portsmouth were also subject to attack. A direct attack on Middle Wallop came on 13 August, resulting in the scrambling of 238 Squadron, as well as 152 and 609 Squadrons from Warmwell. At Middle Wallop the alarm was sounding as Ju 87 Stukas and a Ju 88 bombed the airfield. No. 238 Squadron sustained the loss of four Hurricanes and a pilot was killed. On the following day another attack on Middle Wallop took place with He 111s and Ju 88s bombing the airfield, resulting in hangars 4 and 5 being hit. Three civilians in a shelter were also killed and others were injured while seeking to close the doors of a hangar. The bombing resulted in fires and the air was rent by the sound of exploding ammunition. Two Spitfires from 609 Squadron brought down an attacking aircraft. Attacks continued after 609 had managed to land for more ammunition and fuel at 5.15 pm. Arriving late, one of the 609 Squadron planes attacked an He 111 that was weaving to avoid detection, causing it to crash. The next day, 15 August, saw all four of the squadrons based at Middle Wallop in action with losses to both the RAF and the Luftwaffe.

Enemy aircraft returned to Middle Wallop on 15 August, enjoying the good weather over the British Isles in an attack on both radar and airfields. Middle Wallop was not attacked until early evening when hangars 4 and 5 were once again targeted. No. 609 Squadron had been scrambled in time to mount a counter-attack on the Luftwaffe, shooting down a Ju 88 and three Me 110s, as well as achieving three probable kills. In the early evening twelve German aircraft departing from a base in Paris flew in low and simultaneously dropped their bombs with hangars 4 and 5 yet again bearing the brunt of the attack. What with the great sound of AA fire and exploding bombs, the noise was deafening for anyone working in the operations room. On that day three Spitfires were lost from 152 Squadron but all their pilots survived. From 234 Squadron, one pilot was killed and after having to ditch in the Channel two others became PoWs. No. 604 Squadron lost a Blenheim destroyed on the ground. Although the numbers shot down were exaggerated by both sides, there was a switch away from daytime attacks by the Germans in response to the heavy losses they had incurred. An indication of weak German navigational skills was that German pilots attacking Middle Wallop were convinced they were attacking Andover, Biggin Hill or Kenley.

The attacks so far had underlined the vulnerability of Middle Wallop's operations room working out of a hut which, as a result of the attacks of 16 August, came perilously close to total destruction. An essential control operation of this kind should have been underground in a blastproof environment. November witnessed the decisive switch in attacks from airfields to London. There is some evidence, however, that a decoy airfield at Broughton lit with flare paths may have saved Middle Wallop from some attacks. On 21 September a Ju 88 operating out of Orléans again bombed the airfield, dropping oil and incendiary bombs close to the operations room and six HE bombs in the proximity of the officers' mess. The Ju 88 was caught by Spitfires and downed in Sussex.

By the end of the Battle of Britain an expanded Middle Wallop was hosting 238 and 56 Squadrons flying Hurricanes. The appearance of a mobile radar caravan containing advanced electronic equipment provided the basis of effective enemy interception GCI (Ground Control Interception) through which a controller was able to guide night-fighters to enemy planes. The success of the system led to additional centres being set up at nearby places such as Sopley.

At Odiham just after the Dunkirk evacuation a range of largely useless planes from Belgium and Holland arrived at Odiham airfield together with airmen from Holland, Belgium and France. Following a visit by General de Gaulle, the decision was made to disperse the aircraft elsewhere. At 9.00 am on 10 August 1940 the Luftwaffe targeted Odiham but were intercepted by Hurricanes from 43 Squadron based at Tangmere. However, three days later, having mistaken Odiham for Andover, the Luftwaffe bombed the airfield on a day when Middle Wallop was also attacked. A combination of AA fire and attacks from Hurricanes and Spitfires resulted in the Ju 88s dropping their bombs outside the airfield. In this twenty-four-hour period the Luftwaffe had flown 1,786 sorties with 520 bombers but still failed to defeat the RAF and left Odiham unscathed.

With the commencement of the Battle of Britain, because of its strategic position Portsmouth airfield was certain to be subject to attack. On 11 July it was bombed, causing damage to the Airspeed Works that were based there. As we will see in discussion of Hampshire's blitz, Portsmouth's strategic vulnerability made it an inappropriate location for fighter aircraft. At Andover despite enemy aircraft regularly passing overhead it was not until 13 August that the airfield was identified as a target. Five low-flying Ju 88s dropped bombs on the airfield's headquarters, parade ground and landing area, resulting in three deaths and damage to six Blenheims. Andover had a decoy airfield 7 miles away at Hursthourne that was unfortunately established too late to divert an attacking aircraft from dropping anti-personnel bombs that killed two people. The first attack on Farnborough took place on 2 August 1940, a clear indication that the Germans had registered its strategic importance. A second attack directed at Farnborough failed to arrive at the RAE. Finally on 16 August eight Ju 88s dropped twenty HE bombs on the RAE. Early warning had been given but a bomb penetrated one of the shelters, killing three people and injuring several more. When RAE workers came out from the other shelters desperate attempts were made to pull the bricks and masonry away from the shelter in order to reach the dead and injured. Those killed were RAE members of staff A.R. Dixon, J.W.E. Parkhurst and V.G.A. Shefford, who were also members of the Local Defence Force. The work of the RAE was seriously disrupted for several days but it slowly returned to normal operation. At this stage of the Battle of Britain the Germans believed that Britain had only 300 serviceable aircraft when in fact 700 were available. The grave concern, however, was the lack of pilots. Farnborough came forward with help by creating its own defence flight with a Spitfire, two Hurricanes and a Gladiator.

When it became apparent that global conflict was engulfing Europe, Gosport went through a process of expansion with grass runways replacing its tarmac surfaces. Tarmac had existed because of the practice required for planes operating off carriers to land and airmen needed to practise landings on a surface of this kind. The airfield became a centre for the testing of planes carrying torpedoes. During the 'Phoney War' Gosport continued its role in training. On 12 August Gosport was attacked, resulting in severe cratering of its runways. Later in the evening the Luftwaffe returned as part of an attack that included the radar masts at Ventnor on the Isle of Wight. The next attack on 16 August resulted in the loss of Skuas and Rocs lined up on the airfield. Four men were killed, two seriously injured and many sustained minor injuries. On 18 August, referred to as the hardest day of the Battle of Britain, in the midst of repairing the airfield from the attack of 16 August, dive-bombers again attacked Gosport, this time destroying engineering workshops, two additional hangars and the motor transport section with parked vehicles as well as several aircraft. This time repairs took longer with new hangars having to be constructed, resulting in the airfield not being able to receive a resident squadron until December 1940. At Lee-on-Solent 778 Squadron had been formed in late 1939. On 16 August there was a major attack on the airfield whose only defence was inadequate Lewis guns. There were two direct hits on the hangars destroying all the aircraft inside, while those outside became buckled pieces of wreckage.

In the early evening of 9 September 1940, a critical moment was being enacted in the skies above Aldershot. Enemy He 111s were spotted and 605 Squadron flying Hurricane 1s rushed to engage them. Pilot Officer Humphries, a New Zealander with half his cockpit shot away, was forced to ditch his plane near the railway line at Bentley. Although he was wounded, he managed to bail out safely. Not so fortunate was a Hurricane flown by Pilot Officer Forester who was caught in crossfire from machine guns and was killed when his plane crashed a short distance from Alton.

Brothers Patrick and Tony Woods-Scawen were two local tearaways who enjoyed racing around the Farnborough area on their motorbikes. Their preoccupation was with speed, no matter how dangerous that might be, as they raced past Blackbushe Airfield on the A30. They joined the RAF, Patrick in October 1937 and his brother some time later on a short-service commission. Unfortunately Tony suffered from very poor eyesight so in order to pass his medical he memorized the letters on the eyesight test. He had glasses fitted into his goggles and in his squadron he earned the nickname of 'wombat'. He joined 43 Squadron and was involved in action above Dunkirk where he claimed his first kill. However, on 31 May 1940 his plane was hit, resulting in a crash-landing prior to his return to Tangmere. After Dunkirk he was almost constantly in action, having to bail out on 7 June after being hit by German aircraft over enemy territory where he successfully evaded capture. By August there was evidence that he was having problems with his eyesight and although he claimed successes he was shot down on 2 September 1940 for the fifth time over Sussex at too low an altitude for his parachute to work effectively and he was killed.

During May 1940 Patrick Woods-Scawen destroyed six enemy aircraft and was involved in the destruction of others. On 19 May he was confronted with a heavy concentration of German aircraft and although heavily outnumbered did not hesitate to attack. On 1 September his own plane was crippled by Bf 109s, forcing him to bail out over Caterham in Kent. Unfortunately his parachute failed to open and he was killed. His body was not found for four days and meanwhile the day after he was reported missing, his brother Tony was killed just twenty-four hours after Patrick's death.

Summing up the experience of the pilots of the Spitfires and Hurricanes, former pilot Peter Hairs said: 'It was a question of just piling in, trying to pick out a target and trying to shoot it. Then you found someone was shooting at you.' Certainly this was a terse response, disguising true valour.

View of the cockpit of an Allied bomber.

*Molly Rose, one of the pioneer female pilots who
delivered new aircraft to airfields.*

Work on Spitfires at Supermarine. The production rate exceeded that of Germany in aircraft manufacture.

Wing Commander Currant, DSO, DFC and Bar, commander at Ibsley.

CHAPTER ELEVEN

Hampshire and Radar

From the time of Watson-Watts' invention of radar in 1933 to the establishment of the chain of radar defence, radar became recognized as a vital element in the defence of Britain from aerial attack. In 1936 Air Chief Marshal Hugh Dowding recognized the immense value of radar and ordered the construction of a metal tower at Stanmore. Watson-Watt analysed the challenge of radar as being how the information it provided was interpreted. A chain system had been established by 1940 where information was passed down a chain of command. Chain Home Low radar was brought into action in reaction to low-flying attacks having the benefit of sweeping the coastline at a lower level. Construction of a radar centre at Ventnor on the Isle of Wight was held up due to local reluctance to part with the necessary land. It consisted of a 360ft tower powered from the national grid. When war was declared on 3 September all twenty stations were operating. After Dunkirk, the radar system around the British coast provided vital intelligence about Luftwaffe attack from planes from occupied northern France. In 1940 there were twenty-one operational radar chain stations and twenty sound mirrors, concrete slabs of doubtful value because they went out of action in bad weather. It quickly became apparent that the existing system struggled to detect low-flying aircraft. Here the Observer Corps that had originated in the Great War played a key role in filling the gaps in intelligence. The corps was recalled into existence at Winchester on 12 August 1938.

Experimental development in on-plane radar was pioneered at Southbourne, Sopley and Middle Wallop. There was testing of type 282 radar at HMS *Eastney* and HMS *Mercury* based in Petersfield. At Gosport experimental work on radar associated with AA batteries was developed. An army radar unit working on a system of ground-control interception offering scrutiny at 360 degrees was pioneered at Christchurch. The prototype was set up at Sopley in the Avon Valley and was soon in operation using the call sign 'Starlight'. The RAE at Farnborough built one of the prototypes which had the added virtue of being mobile and able to be mounted on trucks. Mary Emery from Nursling worked as a radar operator, which involved maintaining the radar transmitter, cleaning the power unit and checking it was topped up with fuel and continuously searching the skies for enemy planes. She recalled: 'When we weren't on duty we would have dances.' These were attended by sailors docked in Southampton and Portsmouth. She and her colleagues detected that the Germans were dropping 'chaff' (thin strips of aluminium foil or similar) as a countermeasure; this would result in confusing multiple radar readings of false targets. She claimed that, coming from women, their observations were disregarded until the same effect was also detected at other stations.

CHAPTER TWELVE

Hampshire and the Blitz

One of the author's classmates in New Zealand was known as 'Chorus Cook' because he was a rocker and sang in a rock band. One time he somehow started talking about his early life in Southampton and his experience of the blitz before his family emigrated to Christchurch. Out of the blue his eyes moistened and he cried. I had vaguely heard of bombing in the war but never realized the deep scars left on many of those who experienced it. Mrs Joyce Carlisle, who was working at Wellworthys during the war, says that to the blitz – which affected everyone along the south coast – was added the sinking of HMS *Hood* in 1941. 'So many of the 1,415 men who were killed were young men from our area,' said Mrs Carlisle. They are remembered in a chapel at Boldre and at the Naval Museum in Portsmouth.

The experience of the attacks on Hampshire by the Luftwaffe varied dramatically according to where one lived in proximity to strategic wartime targets. Even then, due to weaknesses in German intelligence, where bombing actually occurred could be of a random nature. If the term 'blitz' has any real meaning for Hampshire, it must be in the context of the bombing of Portsmouth, Gosport and Southampton in 1940 and 1941. The term has come to have an immediate association with saturation bombing of parts of London and what happened to these urban centres in Hampshire is somewhat neglected. This is surprising considering the concentration of naval and defence manufacturing activity in this area which was certain to draw down attack by the Germans. Furthermore, of the two cities bombed during the blitz the suffering and privation experienced by the people of Portsmouth seemed more catastrophic than that of Southampton. For this reason, the experience of the blitz in Portsmouth will be examined first.

The official book on the blitz in Portsmouth refers to it as the 'Smitten City' and by the time the Luftwaffe had finished its trail of destruction that was not an overstatement. Between 6 July 1940 and May 1944 it endured sixty-seven raids. Life became a constant succession of sirens wailing with 1,581 alerts and being subjected to 1,320 high-explosive bombs, 38,000 incendiaries and 38,000 parachute bombs. Nearly 1,000 civilians were killed, 1,216 were injured requiring hospital attention and a further 1,621 sustained lesser injuries. Portsmouth also sustained city-wide structural damage. This included the destruction of its Guildhall, 8 schools, 30 churches, 1 hospital, 4 cinemas, 1 music hall and 211 pubs and other licensed premises. In terms of

Bomb damage in Bournemouth.

property, 6,625 homes were destroyed, 6,549 seriously damaged and 69,886 slightly damaged.

The first night of the blitz on 6 July 1940 saw bombing continue for four hours. It was a concentrated raid but on that night casualties were fortunately light. The Luftwaffe managed to achieve some damage to military targets, and civic targets such as a nursing home and a brewery were destroyed. The following night the raiders reappeared, this time for an attack lasting six hours. Casualties this time were 93 killed with another 250 injured. Buildings destroyed included the Royal Sailors' Home Club, the synagogue and Keppel's Head Hotel. On another night twenty-one were killed and forty-eight injured. The bombing resulted in the decimation of much of the city's architectural heritage such as St Matthew's Church in Southsea and the Royal Garrison Church where King James II had worshipped and King Charles II had married Catherine of Braganza. On 6 February 1941 the king and queen made an exhaustive tour of the areas of Portsmouth that had suffered most. The royal couple took the time to talk directly to residents who had endured the worst of the bombing.

On 10 January 1941 the bombing of Portsmouth's Guildhall seemed to strike at the very heart of the city, for here was located the strategic centre for all the planning of how to cope with an attack on this scale. Its roof collapsed after three showers of incendiary bombs fell on it. The Lord Mayor and ARP personnel barely had time to make their escape. Throughout the following day flames were seen spiralling out of the Guildhall's 200ft high tower when it blazed like a torch, melting its copper plates so that they fell into the interior of the building. Lost were all the Guildhall's pictures, its renowned walnut panelling, its mosaic pavement, a valuable organ and all Portsmouth's civic possessions. Saved, however, were its Bodkin loving cup and the mayor's mace presented to the city in 1658. At this time Portsmouth's main shopping area along Palmerston Road, King's Road and Commercial Road was gutted. There were 2,314 separate fires, 3,000 people were left homeless, 171 killed and 430 injured. Large parts of the city's civic fabric were destroyed on 10 January including Clarence Pier, the Hippodrome, the Dockyard School, the Connaught Drill Hall and the Royal Sailors' Rest.

Although the Germans strategically claimed that their attacks were on naval targets, Portsmouth's residential areas seemed to suffer disproportionately. On 11 July 1940 the Blue Anchor Hotel was hit and a large hole was blown in the gas holder at Rudmore. There was a direct hit on the ARP and first-aid station at Drayton School. Twenty bombs killed nineteen people and injured eighty, many of whom were in a serious condition. As the tempo of raids intensified, so too did the scramble to convert cellars and basements and provide water tanks for effective fire-fighting. It was expected that everyone would do their duty in fire-watching as part of their contribution to the war effort. Unfortunately the dominant feature of the early raids was one of disorganization featuring elements of panic and families trekking out of the city. Fortunately for people who were spending nights under hedges, the raids coincided with a warm summer. Fleeing by motor car was not possible due to petrol rationing, and because lights on cars were heavily masked, driving at night was hazardous anyway. Trains had to be dispersed to sidings away from stations to avoid attack.

On 13 August 1940, *Adlertag* – 'Eagle Day', the first day of the German Operation EAGLE ATTACK (*Unternehmen Adlergriff*) – there was a mass attack on the dockyard during which the floating crane alongside the *Queen Elizabeth* was badly damaged. Fortunately a bomb missed the sailors' quarters by a matter of yards and a 500lb bomb crashed through the roof of the wardroom without exploding. A third raid on 24 August by twenty-four Ju 88s with sixty-five delayed-action bombs concentrated on Portsmouth and Southsea, resulting in 117 killed, 1,100 badly injured and 500 rendered homeless. Buildings destroyed included the Princess Theatre where a children's performance was taking place, killing eight and injuring seventeen. There was a direct hit on a shelter that killed twenty-five and injured another forty. The author William Golding reported seeing a petty officer standing up in the middle of the raid to illustrate to new recruits how safe it was during a raid. Bombing of the Carlton Cinema in Cosham resulted in 44 deaths and 140 injuries.

There were two more raids in August, five in September and thirty by the end of 1940. On 9 March 1941 there was a four-hour raid aimed at naval targets, and on 10 March a six-hour raid resulting in 120 dead and 300 injured. Admiralty House was hit but the bomb did not explode; this resulted in Admiral Jones moving his headquarters to HMS *Victory*. On 31 January Churchill toured the battered city with Harry Hopkins, the American Secretary of State. April brought another month of raids, notably on the 8th and 27th. Throughout the war the Portsmouth area had to suffer the consequences of German raiders jettisoning their unused bombs after raids inland. Portsmouth was forced to witness the destruction of buildings that had taken many years to build being destroyed within a few seconds.

The perspective of those caught in these bombing raids was given by Anne Joseph, who described being in a Morrison shelter in her family's house in Havant as like being in a cage: 'Ours was set in the corner of the dining room and as the youngest I had to crawl in first and move over to the far wall. It was airless, very hot, and excruciatingly claustrophobic.' Because the family hated their shelter so much, they decided to take their chances in the dining room. When they heard the sound of bombs, her parents would throw themselves on top of Anne and her sister. However, neighbours subsequently advised them of the whereabouts of an Anderson shelter. After a raid one night her father tried to disguise the destruction in Portsmouth as an indication of bad weather in order to protect Anne and her sister from the reality of the bombing.

Sheila Luff's mother was South African by birth but came to Portsmouth to train as a nurse. She was working in a hospital when the bombers arrived. She told the story of a particular night when she was in a building that had supposedly been bomb-proofed. When the alarms went off they decided to sit tight and wait until they were called out. Closer and closer came the sound of the engines of the German planes until they realized that the sound of the crump of bombs indicated they were very near. There came a massive blast that picked up her mother's chair, carrying her down the middle of the building and dropping her, still on the chair, in the middle of the floor. Another blast at the other end of the building did the same thing in reverse.

What was it like to have been bombed out? Someone referring to it in the BBC *WW2 People's War* under the non de plume 'Bathbrick' said that it gave you a certain status. Relatives and friends gathered round with sympathy, food, shelter and even furniture. It was all right to talk about rationing but discussion about the bombing was forbidden. At school in the school certificate year the sound of the sirens was cheered because it meant the lessons could be skipped. Although the government had suggested evacuation up to age 16, this could be resisted by parents. Rumours went around Portsmouth that the bombs being dropped were British bombs captured by the Germans after

Dunkirk. Someone bombed out said: 'At least the bombs that did it were British bombs.' In January 1940 one boy had taken shelter in the basement of a big department store and after the sound of the bombs falling it became eerily silent. His parents ventured upstairs only to discover the whole building was on fire. The shop owned by his parents was still standing but goods from it were strewn all over the road. In the pub opposite the landlady clutching her cash register was refusing to leave until his mother persuaded her to do so. The boy's parents had an arrangement to meet at a shelter halfway to Old Portsmouth. He cycled to the common where the shelter was located, only to discover that it was so full he had to stand by the door. The common was surrounded by fire and there was complete dereliction. His parents' shop was also a lending library. They were contemplating the ruins of the shop when a friend appeared and asked if he could borrow a book after looking at them spread across the road. Their house itself was a pile of rubble; all that was left by a high-explosive bomb after the raid. Like many in the city, his family then set out to walk to a friend's house to find shelter, his mother carrying a small bag containing important family documents. Then it was off to Maidenhead and shelter from other relatives, the only thing coming from the government being a clothing grant. Just forty-eight hours after losing everything in their house, his mum and dad were dancing in the local pub at Marlow.

As the war continued into 1941 a fire blitz in January resulted in a concrete command post rocking like a ship at sea. On 10 March a direct hit on 215 Battery resulted in the deaths of eleven men. On 17 April, at 219 Battery on Hayling Island six men were killed and another thirty injured. A shower of incendiaries had lit up the gun and the bombers clustered around it like moths to a flame. Development in radar based at Portsdown enabled guns on the Solent to fire 1,420 rounds at attacking planes and succeeding in shooting down four of them. A problem arose when experienced gunners were sent overseas, so some of their roles were taken over by women.

As far as Gosport was concerned, in November 1940 an attack using hundreds of incendiary bombs resulted in the destruction of the officers' mess and whole areas of stores covering 200 sq. ft, causing the death of one person and a rating. In March 1941 two 500lb bombs were dropped at the gun factory. One man caught by the consequences of an incendiary bomb was described as burning like a human torch. In a hospital bed next to him a young man with severe burns was in so much pain he called out for someone to shoot him. A direct hit on a major printing works resulted in its paper burning for two weeks. There were 1,591 alerts in Gosport and 61 raids which left 111 dead with 70 seriously injured and 219 having minor injuries. As far as Gosport's level of bombing was concerned, high explosives numbered 411, and 10,000 incendiaries were dropped causing major damage to 933 properties and slight damage to 10,866. Gosport's heaviest raids were on 12 and 16 August 1940 and 10 January, 10 March and 14 June 1941.

Sporadic bombing attacks in the Aldershot area often had severe consequences reflective of its key military role. The first attack on the Guillemot Barracks on 6 July 1940 by a single Heinkel bomber at 4.15 resulted in the destruction of two cottages, seven deaths and many injuries. The Canadians based nearby helped in the rescue operation. Moving south, the same plane attacked the Wellington Lines 4 miles away, dropping bombs on the parade ground which was crowded with soldiers, killing three and injuring thirty. Obviously Farnborough with its airfield and well-known role in support of aircraft testing and production was a prime target. The first attempted raid against the RAE by the Luftwaffe on 2 August 1940 was scared off by the RAF. However, on 16 August 1940 six Ju 88s dropped twenty high-explosive bombs hitting an anti-aircraft battery, with ten of them damaging the RAE's test bed. There were three deaths among the local defence force sheltering nearby. Nevertheless, the result of the attack only delayed work at the RAE by three days. On 22 August a train carrying a large supply of ammunition halted at Tongham was attacked and set on fire with spectacular visual consequences. In Farnborough there were two raids, killing three people including a Canadian soldier.

Southampton was a prime target for attack as an important port complex with an industrial base, a major railway complex with carriage and locomotive work at nearby Eastleigh. At Vospers RAF rescue boats were being built and power boats were being constructed at Hythe. As well as building Spitfires, Supermarine was also involved in the construction of seaplanes. A whole complex of aviation activity was in place around Hamble aerodrome with a switch from construction of airliners to building bombers.

On 20 June the first raid occurred at Millbrook, resulting in the deaths of six people. An advert for the Longdown Hotel offered a secure, comfortable and very efficient air-raid shelter. Despite moves to mobilize auxiliary fire services, the WRVS and other voluntary organizations, the first raids brought with them an element of panic. The summer and autumn raids resulted in the almost complete obliteration of Southampton Civic Centre with 481 deaths from enemy action. Audrey Hunt was in the Arts Centre on 6 November 1940 when it received a direct hit at 2.30 pm. In the basement of the school where the students had taken shelter the collapse of the building resulted in them being buried alive under tons of concrete and she was the only one to survive. Mrs Udell, who was just 18 at the time, remembered the heavy raid of 23 November and having to deal with the incendiaries that were dropped on her home in the absence of her parents: 'The siren went and enemy planes were overhead and immediately incendiaries began falling, two landing in our garden. Frantic with fear, I went out with a stirrup pump. I was alone in our street because our neighbours had fled to the country.' While she was running between her house and their shelter she heard the glass in one of the windows crashing down behind her. Between 30 November 1940 and 1 December

1941, 800 high explosives and 9,000 incendiaries were dropped on the city. John Totlas, who worked in a factory making parts for aero engines, was out with his fiancée at the Royal Cinema on Saturday, 30 November. When the siren sounded the manager suggested that the audience should leave in small groups. They were on the balcony, so they moved to the stalls. When they emerged it proved difficult to find a bus home amid the damage in Above Bar which was still in flames. The bus John finally located had people lying on the floor as he observed people being carried out of buildings to be taken to hospital. Mrs Drew described how she wept when she saw the destruction of Southampton's churches. Holyrood church was a smoking ruin, St Mary's was gutted and only St Michael's survived. Only the basement remained at Woolworths and Edwin Jones. Mrs Eaton, who was sent to one of the only Post Offices that was open, passed a gentleman who raised his hat and wished her 'Good morning.' He was none other than King George VI.

There were fifty-seven large-scale raids on Southampton but it was the 1,500 almost constant alarms that undermined the morale of the city. Heavy bombardment amounting to 2,300 bombs and over 470 tons of high explosives laid waste to whole parts of the city with 45,000 properties either damaged or destroyed, much of it as a result of fire from incendiary bombs. Fires in the city were visible in Cherbourg. Undoubtedly the worst raids were on 23 and 30 November and 1 December 1940. With the last raid of fifty bombers in July 1943, the worst was over. The death toll was 630 with 898 seriously wounded and thousands with minor injuries. All this made Southampton the seventh heaviest-bombed city in England.

Legends abound regarding the ferocity of the bombing. One of these is the bombing of the international cold store on the docks with its huge store of 2,300 tons of butter that burned for nine days. From 20 June the Luftwaffe ratcheted up their attacks, culminating in three major raids at the end of November 1940 commencing at 6.30 in the evening and lasting from five to seven hours. Some 2,000 firemen tackled the fires, many drawn from other parts of Hampshire. On 15 September thirty German aircraft attacked the Supermarine factory, dropping 12 tons of bombs. This was followed on the 24th by another attack on Supermarine when 200 bombs were dropped, killing fifty-five and forcing production to be moved away to alternative sites such as Castle Bromwich. In the city a direct hit on an Anderson shelter left it covered in body parts. On 23 November commencing at 6.15 pm the dropping of 4,000 incendiaries killed 77 people and injured 300. A direct hit on a shelter resulted in only two survivors out of the thirty people taking refuge. Despite the opening of fifteen emergency centres, 4,000 people fled the city.

John Cary in Portsmouth described the two shelters used by the family: a cupboard under the stairs and an Anderson shelter in the garden. The Anderson shelter was cold, wet and lit by a paraffin lamp. His memory is one of almost permanent fear. Molly Lang remembered a two days on/two days off working regime at Fort Southwick and being permanently tired. As the war went on, less and less notice was given to take her typewriter down to the shelter and continue working there. John Dean was an auxiliary fireman at the power station and remembered the night a bomb dropped through its roof. There then followed a desperate struggle to get the three turbines working again while around them the docks were ablaze. Incendiary bombs set alight the stores of coal, despite sailors working desperately to pull them out of harm's way. Following the raid of 10 January 1940, bodies were laid on the pavement outside the barracks and armed guards deployed everywhere to prevent looting. John believed that land mines were the worst. Each night the buses were packed as people left Portsmouth for the chalk pits at Rowlands Castle. It was difficult to use private transport because petrol was rationed to 3 gallons per month. However, research that took place on 14 March 1941 found that even after the terrors of the blitz, only 75 per cent of women and children wanted to evacuate and that children who had been evacuated were often in a more nervous state than those who had stayed behind. Families, and that usually meant women, faced considerable domestic difficulties in dealing with things like fuel shortages when the gas supply was lost and windows had been broken during raids, together with getting other damage to their houses repaired. Public shelters were in short supply and in some cases those designed for 50 people were accommodating more than 100.

Matthew Harvey, whose father was vice principal of the Art College and who was killed when it was bombed, related the bombing of the house next door to them. Fortunately the two boys who lived in the house were staying with them and were in their shelter. For their mother, who had already lost her husband, this was yet another tragedy as their house was so badly damaged that it had to be demolished. John Player had been evacuated to a farm near Fordingbridge. A fellow evacuee was staying in a house where a Heinkel 111 crashed one night, bringing down the plaster in his bedroom. At Southampton's GPO telephone exchange the operators continued to work, despite the fact that incendiary bombs had been dropped on the building's roof. At the end of December 1940 Sue Language wrote that

> surely the city had a right to some peace bearing in mind the pounding it had received during the preceding nights. The remaining large departmental store, which had enormous stocks of foodstuffs and general supplies, is completely burned to the ground… there is hardly a shop left in the High Street.

She reported that fire engines from as far afield as London and Wells had been grappling with the fires caused by incendiary bombs but saw casualties being taken from a shelter that had received a direct hit. Pauline Miles described how she drove back into the street where her family lived and heard her father exclaim 'It's gone!' on seeing firemen playing water on the flaming remains of where their flat had once stood. She remembered standing on the pavement and screaming out the names of her dolls for them to come out to her. All her family's possessions had been lost and they were then in B&B accommodation for some time.

PC Goronwy Evans recalls the first raid on Portsmouth on 11 July resulting in only minor damage to the dockyard but extensive damage to the north end of the city. There were nineteen deaths including that of a policeman. He recalled Stukas machine-gunning the barrage balloons. Stress was placed on police officers by requiring them to report back to their stations when they were not on shifts each time there was a raid. Because of this, policemen were allocated billets throughout Portsmouth. On 10 March 1940 PC Evans went to a house where the back had been destroyed but the front was burning fiercely. Local residents formed a human chain with buckets of water working to quench the fire which was in danger of spreading to a nearby nursing home. With a stirrup pump he entered the building and put the fire out, thus preventing it from spreading further. For his gallant effort he was rewarded with the George Cross. In 1942 he joined the army and was posted to the Royal Armoured Corps in Farnborough where he qualified as a gunnery instructor. Arthur Harvey, aged just 16 on 24 August 1940, was fire-watching in Portsmouth and recalled bombs falling on the Tramway Arms and commented that the likelihood of death became part of everyday existence. He says of his eight school friends that only four survived the war. Sidney Ties was part of a relief group brought into Portsmouth at the worst stage of its blitz:

> We had no need of lights because the whole city was ablaze. The roads were covered with debris and fire hoses. I saw a bus that had been thrown into a building by a bomb blast. There was a bomb lodged beneath a hospital and we had to evacuate the hospital. Working there I didn't take my clothes off for days that seemed to merge into one.

The attack of 11 July was aimed at French destroyers in the docks but the Me 110 bombs straddled them and this time naval facilities suffered little. The same could not be said of Portsmouth's densely-populated civilian areas where people were caught in the streets. Drayton Road School, which doubled as a first-aid post, witnessed nineteen deaths and twenty-six serious injuries. On 11 July parts of Portsea and Old Portsmouth with flimsily-built houses suffered considerable damage. The members of the RAF team managing the barrage balloon were all killed. Parts of the Harbour Station were destroyed along with three trains. On 12 August 150 Me 109s and 110s roamed Portsmouth and dive-bombed the dockyard. South Portsmouth was attacked by twenty Ju 88s bombing from 1,000ft. The bombs aimed at the *Queen Elizabeth* missed but fell in the roadway, severing water, gas and telephone lines.

Bournemouth had to wait until 23 May 1943 for its worst raid. It was a warm spring morning and the centre of the town was crowded. There had been forty-seven previous incidents but nothing on the scale of what happened that morning. It resulted in 131 deaths plus hundreds of injuries, and 3,359 damaged buildings of which 39 had to be demolished. Two landmark buildings – the Metropole at the Lansdowne and the Central at the bottom of Richmond Hill – lay in ruins. This was a carefully-planned and targeted raid designed to achieve its target quickly and be back at the Germans' base in Caen before any retaliation by the RAF was possible. Whereas a warning of twenty-two minutes was expected in the town, there were only six minutes' warning of this raid. As well as strafing the Pleasure Gardens, twenty-five high-explosive bombs were also dropped.

Hundreds of Canadian airmen were staying at the Metropole Hotel and the Central was packed with Australians. The latter was also a major convalescent centre for injured airmen. The German attack came in the context of the Dam Buster raids which had killed scores of civilians in the resultant flooding and was based on killing airmen who, unlike planes, were difficult to replace. Windows were machine-gunned in Old Christchurch Road and there were direct hits on Beales' department store and West's cinema. However, the greatest loss of life occurred in the Central Hotel where fifty-four were killed including seven Australians and six Americans who were on leave in Bournemouth. Members of the civil defence group meeting at the Central Hotel also perished. Hardly any of Bournemouth's distinctive buildings were spared during the attack. A concert by the Bournemouth Municipal Orchestra was due to take place in the Winter Gardens that night. To have cancelled it would have handed the Germans an excellent propaganda weapon so it went ahead featuring Elgar's *Nimrod* in memory of those who had died. Pamela Lee described how a large land mine parachuted into her road in Bournemouth at 3.35 am on 6 November 1940, hitting a school on the corner where French soldiers were billeted. The blast sucked out all the glass in the windows facing the school and bringing the ceiling down in the house. The Stead family who lived in Holdenhurst Road in Bournemouth was part of a whole culture of fire-watching associated with bombing in the town. One mother of the bride at a wedding upbraided the photographer at the wedding for switching his camera from the happy couple to capturing a low-flying bomber passing over the church.

Doreen Bennett described getting used to the blackout and doing her homework by candlelight. She spoke about the patriotism of herself and the group of young women with whom she shared her billet. Despite the difficulties they were experiencing in having to switch from school classrooms to church halls and sitting on the grass, they were remarkably self-disciplined in their attitude to study. She enrolled at the School of Art in Southampton where she was constantly aware of enemy and Allied aircraft and observed the bombing of Pickfords' cold storage at Totton where bombing had the effect of igniting the tar on the roads, causing it to rise as a mist throughout their suburb. At the School of Art it was usual for the students to seek shelter in its basement. However, on 6 November a decision was made that students would not retreat to the basement on this occasion when the alarm sounded. Unfortunately three bombs fell directly on the school. The room she was in filled with choking dust and smoke and the students joined hands to find a way out in the darkness. They climbed over the rubble and made their way home, unaware at this time that two girls in her class had been killed. The next day Doreen went back to recover her bicycle but it was just a tangled mass of metal. From 20 November she witnessed almost constant bombing in Southampton with firemen having to drain the ponds on the common when the supply of water to quench the fires ran out. Much damage was caused by bombers dropping a stick of bombs on the way back from bombing inland. Electricity and gas supplies were disrupted and water regularly had to be boiled. Ida Pressley described how one night when she was hurrying home, someone at the door of a shelter offered her a place in there during the alert but she declined the offer. Just a few minutes later the shelter received a direct hit and everyone in it was killed. A Mass Observation report on 9 December 1940 found that morale in Southampton had deteriorated and there was a feeling that too little action had been taken to repair essential services. Such was the extent of the damage, there was a feeling that Southampton was finished as a city.

However, during 1941 the RAF developed anti-aircraft sites in the Southampton area at Marlpit Oak and Hag Hill near Wootton Bridge. Each of these gun pits contained three guns and within its earth walls were gun crew rooms, sleeping quarters and ammunition pits, all well camouflaged. When the guns were firing shrapnel cascaded down in the nearby area. A number of examples of devotion to duty arose during the worst of the bombing. One of these was the work of the Ordnance Survey whose 1,500 staff continued to provide vitally important maps throughout the blitz.

On 23 August 1940 in New Milton on the edge of the New Forest, Rose Perrot, a telephone operator at the town's exchange, took a call from Lymington that enemy aircraft were active in the area. Members of the Lancashire Fusiliers risked their lives in running down the main street urging people to take cover. One commentator remembered seeing a lone Heinkel 111 flying over the centre of the town and thinking at first that it was just dropping leaflets. In fact it dropped three 250lb bombs and nineteen anti-personnel incendiaries. These devastated the town centre, killing twenty civilians and five soldiers. Among the dead were Archie Bursey, a telegram boy working at the Post Office delivering telegrams; Alfred Probert who was riding his motorbike accompanied by his wife and their 4-year-old daughter in a sidecar; and Corporal Thomas Davies of the Lancashire Fusiliers who with his wife was on leave when they were killed in Station Road. The Heinkel bomber was flying so low that the German pilot and crew were visible from the ground. There were a further two raids in New Milton in 1942 and another in 1943.

Pauline Colcutt was aged just 7 when the war began and was evacuated from Romsey to Swanage. However, even there it was not safe because one day she saw two orange-nosed German planes flying across the harbour to bomb the town. The children fled their school playground for garden sheds while the planes machine-gunned the area. Recalling the blitz in Eastleigh in August 1941 as a 9-year-old boy, one man remembered a German plane swooping from the sky, its guns blazing and bullets bouncing along the road and the walls around him. He saw a plane taking off from Eastleigh airport in response to the attack and its wing catching a barrage balloon that had just been launched. The result was that it crashed into houses, killing the pilot and his crew. Roy Pidgeon remembered marching down the road with the boys from his school when the siren sounded to go to the air-raid shelter with anti-aircraft guns firing over his head. At home the shelter had single brick veneer walls which did not offer genuine protection. Their shelter had an escape hatch that could be propped open during a raid, enabling a view of what was happening. He was then evacuated to family friends in Christchurch. At Chandler's Ford in the earliest months of the blitz more casualties appeared to have been caused by British planes crashing than by German bombs. On 15 August a British plane crashed onto a house, killing at least three people on the ground as well as seven members of the crew. A Hudson aircraft returning to base with pilots who had ferried planes to Eastleigh airport hit the cable of a barrage balloon and crashed into council houses, killing their occupants as well as the nine people on the plane.

When Cunliffe's Southampton factory was bombed, an ambulance was sent from Eastleigh. On 8 October three HE bombs were dropped on the canteen at the Pirelli Works, a Ju 88 flew low over the town bombing and machine-gunning, resulting in four killed and a further four wounded. Bombs were dropped in the Market and High Streets, Stubbington High Street, Grantham Road and Desborough Road. On the following day two RAF personnel were killed and four injured when an unexploded bomb detonated at the railway running shed. On 30 November Eastleigh again contributed help in dealing with large enemy attacks on Southampton and as attacks continued more ambulance and fire engine support was sent to Thorneycroft and Supermarine. The 11 September bombing of Supermarine was notable for the way in which staff working on the Spitfire continued to work although they knew danger was near. When the bombs fell, staff ran for their lives after most of the aircraft hangar in which they were working crashed around them. Dorothy Inglis recalled her boss pushing her under a desk before they ran for their lives, dodging machine-gun bullets. Winifred Hooper recalled a woman in their shelter trying to get them all to sing but after their experience no one felt inclined to do so. Bombs on 25 February killed two and injured another two, while bombs throughout March continued to cost lives. On 22 June 1942 production at Pirelli was halted due to bombing of the rolling mill, the furnace and the fabric building.

The Richardson family recalled a land mine being caught in the trees of Stoke Park and the arrival of the army bomb disposal squad to deal with it. The children in their school were sent to the huge air-raid shelter for gas mask training and they ignored instructions to wear them at all times. Although they had an Anderson shelter that was shared with their next-door neighbour, they hardly ever used it. The Richardsons accommodated two evacuees from Portsmouth, one with a club foot and another with tuberculosis. People of Chandler's Ford opened their houses to some of the victims of bombing in Southampton, one of the most active groups helping the homeless from Gosport and Southampton being the Salvation Army. As winter approached, on 29 October at 5.00 pm there was an attack from twelve Ju 88s supported by Me 109s bombing from 9,000ft resulting in 390 casualties. October was relatively quiet but the bombing continued throughout November and just before Christmas on 23 December another raid resulted in the death or injury of 100 people together with bomb damage leaving 1,500 homeless.

In March 1941 Ben Smith spoke of the attacks on Portsmouth being prompted by the fleet being in the docks. He was at the cinema watching *Jack Benny Rides Again* when an air-raid warning flashed onto the screen. Most people stayed put but then the lights went out and the audience was hustled out of the emergency exits onto the street. The sky was crisscrossed by searchlights and the whole of Portsmouth seemed to be in flames. He returned home to a terrified mother, only to be bundled up in a blanket and taken to a nearby shelter. Once there it was a dispute with his brother over who would have the top bunk, after which they would count the sound of the bombs as they fell with their shrill whistling sound. 'In the shelter there was a sense of fear only blotted out by burying your head under the blankets,' remembered Ben. When the light went out in their Anderson shelter it was terrifying, especially as they could not get out when a bomb exploded nearby. His father, who was off duty from HMS *Daedalus*, managed to clear away the rubble with the help of two air-raid wardens and free the family. His father had witnessed the results of a poorly-constructed shelter being bombed when the blast had killed a whole family. As Ben was being bundled away he thought he heard screams coming from a house on fire where its woman occupant had refused to evacuate to a shelter. His father was suffering from a burst eardrum from an exploding bomb only a matter of yards away from where he had taken shelter.

What of the efforts regarding defence? Claims are made that some planes were brought down by small-arms fire. Naval battalions mounted the AA defences around naval bases supplemented by the Home Guard. Margaret Hunt, in describing her war, explained what it was like being dug out of a house that had taken a direct hit and of being assigned to a gun site on Hayling Island. It was a sea of mud covered with duckboards and the Nissen huts to which they were assigned were freezing cold and with a shortage of drinkable water. They slept on iron beds with hard mattresses kept warm with three grey blankets. They shared their barracks with frogs, field mice, lizards and rats, some of which crawled over them at night. However, there was equality of privation among men attached to the gun site having the same clothes: trousers, helmets, boots, leather jerkins and teddy-bear coats.

From 11 July 1940 to 18 August 1941 there were 792 raids on Portsmouth, an average of two per day. Policemen were working twelve-hour shifts and the demands made on firemen were even harder. When an oil bomb was dropped on Pickfords on 7 October 1940, firemen carried hoses up four flights of stairs while not wearing respirators. Naina Alice Cox told how her uncle died of pneumonia after being repeatedly soaked using stirrup pumps to quench the fires created by bombing. Sheila Foy described how some children arrived back from school to find their homes had gone. During the worst of the raids, lessons often took place in shelters.

The organization of civic defence at Gosport was centred on the town's Town Hall. The lower rooms were strengthened for this purpose with the town clerk's office becoming the telephone exchange. Located in this area were the medical officer of health, the police and senior representatives of the fire service. The four standard air-raid warnings were established: two red signals for standby, green for raid over and white for all-clear. A routine was established involving the shovelling of sand, water buckets made ready for immediate use, front and back doors being unbolted, avoidance of going out onto the street, seeking always to keep a roof over one's head and having a tin bath available to submerge incendiary bombs in water. However, doubts arose about the safety of the Anderson shelters as proved when there were direct hits on them. There were 24,000 of them in Gosport, 800 strengthened basement shelters and 500 communal shelters. Sad stories abound, such as a mother returning home after the bombing of 24 August and entering the family's Anderson shelter to discover the bodies of her husband, their three children and a 2-week-old grandchild. A register was kept of available rooms that were used to accommodate bombed-out families. The shelter scene was one of uncomfortable wooden bunks and the usual dampness. Women would sit knitting and there might be someone who had brought in a piano accordion to accompany singing to disguise just how terrified most of those in the shelter were. The adults would try to conceal this from the children but the expressions on their faces gave them away.

In the late afternoon of 16 August 1940 ten Ju 88s flew over Basingstoke on their way to bomb airfields in Berkshire. Through a break in the clouds the German pilots saw Basingstoke railway and because of this a bomber dropped a stick of bombs on Church Square with another stick falling on Burgess Road. Twelve people died that afternoon including two children. The attack resulted in the complete destruction of twenty-five properties and partial destruction of twenty-five others. In all, seventeen HE bombs were dropped alongside incendiaries, leaving five unexploded bombs to be dealt with. There were 312 alarms during the war with 12 people being killed, 21 seriously injured and 50 suffering minor injuries. The Report Centre in Romsey reveals a diary of aerial attack on the surrounding area. The centre consisted of a controller, a plotter and logger, a telephonist and scouts, all tasked with using telephone connection to record enemy activity. Incidents such as a barrage balloon breaking loose were communicated via code. The night of 14 August 1940 proved an eventful one with the bombing of Middle Wallop airfield killing three workmen and injuring another four. A German plane was downed at East Dean and there were reports of casualties who by 8 o'clock were in Romsey Hospital. The three civilian casualties were taken to Andover Hospital. On 16 August reports were registered of British aircraft coming down and at 3:15 a report of a British pilot parachuting to safety. In September at 11.20 pm reports came in of two bombs at Manor Farm Rectory and three bombs ending up in a local pond; clear evidence that they were bombs being jettisoned by bombers returning from raids. These could be just as lethal as those used in raids, with the bombs dropped at Fernyhurst Rownhams killing three children and slightly injuring three others on 22 June 1941.

In Alton John McKernon remembered seeing a German bomber dropping an incendiary bomb on St Lawrence Infants' School on 17 November 1940. His father ran to the school and had managed to extinguish the incendiary by the time the fire brigade arrived.

Historians still debate the morale of the people of Southampton, Portsmouth and Gosport after the period of saturation bombing endured by them in 1940–41. Certainly the stiff upper lip attributed to these communities' morale by some commentators is seriously disputed by the findings of the Mass Observation Team. Their research quoted in the Oral History Team's findings in *Southampton Blitz – The Official Story* and quoted by Tom Harrison paints a different picture. Following the blitz of 1940–41 they identify a deteriorating morale due to the failure of civic government to 'rally' the inhabitants of bombed-out communities such as Southampton. The report points to serious delays in repairing thousands of buildings partially destroyed by bombing, with broken windows and leaking roofs consigning their inhabitants to a miserable existence. In the absence of electricity there was even a shortage of candles. After a fortnight following the raids, there was an obsession with the experience among a large section of the population which raised questions about their psychological condition. The mitigating factor in this was that the local pub continued to function with its pianist and singer. However, a jaundiced view of the ability of local authorities to provide competent civil leadership was identified. This breakdown in morale was highlighted by Joyce Carlisle who stated that people were so exhausted that they would no longer care if the Germans invaded. In the War Cabinet, Herbert Morrison identified a collapse in morale in Portsmouth, Southampton and Plymouth.

An unexploded bomb with a policeman.

Troops assisting in clearing bomb damage.

Clearing up bomb damage.

Bomb damage at the Hotel Metropole, Bournemouth.

New female recruits to the armed forces.

Woman above an air-raid shelter in Portsmouth.

CHAPTER THIRTEEN

Hampshire's Secret War

'Remember before God those men and women of the European Resistance training in Beaulieu to fight their lonely battle against Hitler's Germany and before entering Nazi-occupied territory here found some measure of the peace for which they fought.' These are the words on the commemorative plaque in Beaulieu Abbey for those who trained at Beaulieu for espionage work in occupied Europe. At Beaulieu 3,000 men and women covering fifteen different nationalities were trained to support resistance in occupied Europe during the Second World War.

Until 1935 there had been a general suspicion about underhand diplomacy and unofficial warfare. However, from this time onwards an interest developed in guerrilla tactics based on those of T.E. Lawrence in Arabia. The validity of stay-behind groups, organizations promoting subversion and sabotage and the promotion of irregular warfare were examined. The progression to setting up training activities was undermined by dispute between the Special Operations Executive (SOE) and the Special Intelligence Executive, the specialized French service, and the SIS (also known as MI6). The forebears of the SOE lay in the military intelligence unit which in 1938 was examining ways to undermine the German economy. Royal Engineer Major J.C.F. Holland was examining how to develop an irregular warfare unit. Churchill was enthusiastic about the potential offered by the embryonic unit and Hugh Dalton, who subsequently became a leading figure in the postwar Labour government, was appointed as its director, tasked by Churchill to 'set Europe ablaze'.

Called 'the Finishing School' for agents, Noreen Baxter-Riols characterized the experience of training at Beaulieu in the New Forest as 'a life of lies'. Residents living cheek-by-jowl with the intense training of these agents were unaware it was happening. Within a few hundred yards from them was a James Bond range of activities that included a convicted bank robber from Glasgow showing how to blow up safes, planting explosives, burglary, sabotage and silent killing. Bizarre activities included planting explosives in rats and a whole raft of devices such as a compass hidden in a hairbrush and a deadly blade in a shoelace. Specialist tutors were brought in such as the king's gamekeeper who provided instruction on how to live off the land.

The students at this spies' training school were about to be initiated into skills as agents which in the case of those training to be wireless operators

Noor Inayat Khan   Peter Lake   Roger Landes

Philippe Liewer   Isidore Newman   Alfred Newton

Henry Newton   Jacques Poirier   Denis Rake

Maurice Southgate   Francis Suttill   Violette Szabo

Some of the agents trained at Beaulieu.

enjoyed a life expectancy of around six weeks. Those recruited as agents were carefully graded and those deemed to lack the necessary skills were isolated in such a way as to prevent them talking about the initial period of instruction they had experienced. There was parachute training in Manchester, followed by Group B schools based in Beaulieu. Only when agents had satisfactorily completed all aspects of this training would they be allowed to go abroad. However, devising anything like effective courses necessary to operate overseas was only achieved through trial and error over a period of two years. This process was made more sophisticated with the creation of a Students Assessment Board based in Cranleigh, Surrey.

In 1940, when France fell, Britain possessed only the rudiments of any way of assisting resistance groups within an enemy country. Little thought had been given to the civilians who wanted to fight back against the Germans and needed Allied help. There was rivalry between the groups who might be looked to for this activity and a new start with a new organization was required. For this reason the Special Operations Executive came into existence in July 1940 and Group B training began to be organized on Lord Montague's Beaulieu estate in the New Forest. Hugh Dalton, the SOE's first director, dismissed the early targets set for the SOE as being too ambitious and it proved difficult to convince military command that the objectives of the SOE were worthwhile. It was found that the Whitley and Wellington planes used for air drops could be too easily intercepted from the ground, so they were replaced with the smaller Lysander. Much time was spent at 'the Finishing School' devising cover stories for agents who were always at great risk of giving themselves away. For example, one agent went into a French café and asked for café noir (black coffee), which immediately blew his cover because all coffee was noir as milk was unavailable.

One notorious name associated with Beaulieu was that of Kim Philby who insisted on following the ten-day training course. The school was staffed by 30 officers, 15 sergeants, 30 NCOs and 175 other ranks. In 1939 Dalton had to start with just fifty officers on which to build the SOE. The school was set up around a whole series of different houses irrespective of nationality, with the Norwegians occupying the various houses at different times. The attrition rate among the trained agents was very high. In April 1942, of the 27 agents parachuted in by the Allies after training at Beaulieu only 2 survived, 9 being executed and 16 tortured in concentration camps. Later in the war, training took place for 400 agents. At Beaulieu Philby was working on a training manual that incorporated the Soviet training he had already followed. In 1940 when the school was beginning, only one of its tutors, Eric Patterson, had actual previous experience of spying. Even by 1941 the tutorial staff consisted of a motley crew of instructors, recruiting agents and linguists. Such was the range of previously criminal skills taught that the Germans nicknamed it 'the Gangster School'. Guy Burgess, the Soviet spy who originally had been associated with the school, was finally sacked in 1940 when his drunken escapades became no longer acceptable to Beaulieu's management.

Beaulieu brought with it a whole host of associated challenges, not least of which was the language competency demanded of all its students. Radio operators for security were required to continually relearn a whole series of codes, with Jacques Doneux – an Englishman of Belgian descent – providing invaluable expertise in this area. The first batch of trainees comprised twenty-five Spaniards who had been trained on the shore of the Solent. One of the trainees, Nigel Lau, turned out to be a con man who disappeared with all the money allocated to support agents in France. Training took place for 400 Norwegians tasked with disabling the heavy water plant in German-occupied northern Norway. Each of the houses incorporated in the Beaulieu complex made a contribution towards the overall training offered. Beaulieu Road Station, the train stop before Brockenhurst, provided top-secret links for agents from occupied countries; at Warren House skills in micro-photography were learned; at the Droukes agents were taught how to make duplicate keys; and other houses specialized in forgery training and safe-breaking. Skills relating to propaganda also had to be taught, such as those required to spread damaging rumours. All the bedrooms of the trainee agents were bugged so that the management was aware of informal comments of students about their training, this being another measure of their suitability. Part of the test of suitability of male operators was how easily they resisted a pretty face. Noreen Baxter, as an 18-year-old, was set up as a man-trap for an agent who easily broke his cover because of their relationship.

Examples exist of the crucial role played by resistance groups in support of D-Day. In France the German Das Reich Division was being rushed to Normandy to reinforce German troops after D-Day. They were delayed for seventeen days in the Toulouse area by SOE-backed ambushes and sabotage. The SOE had put 10,000 tons of arms into France alone during the D-Day period and there were fifty wireless operators providing crucial communication links. The SOE was invaluable in forging a spirit of resistance throughout occupied Europe. In all, 400 agents were sent into countries occupied by the Germans and of these 39 were women. In France, agent Noreen Baxter was stopped by a German officer when carrying a wireless in her basket and asked what she had in the basket. Brazenly she said it was a wireless and she was in contact with London every day. The German simply laughed and said he didn't believe her because she was too lovely to be a spy.

Weapons available to agents at the SOE training centre.

Leslie Howard on the set of The First of the Few *at a Hampshire airfield.*

Loading a bomber at a Hampshire airfield.

CHAPTER FOURTEEN

Hampshire's Airfields

The vital role played by the airfields of Hampshire in the Battle of Britain has been covered. We now turn to the beginning of the fight back and the way in which Hampshire airfields provided landing stages for the bombing of Germany and other strategic targets. A list of these airfields includes RAF Soberton, RAF Stoney Cross, Swanwick, RAF Thorney Island, RAF Andover, RAF Beaulieu, RAF Calshot, RAF Chilbolton, RAF Christchurch, RAF Farnborough, RAF Frost Farm, RAF Gosport (which became HMS *Siskin* in 1945), RAF Hamble, RAF Hartford Bridge (now Blackbushe), RAF Holmsley, RAF Hurn (now Bournemouth International Airport), RAF Ibsley, RAF Lasham, RAF Lee-on-Solent (transferred to the Royal Navy), and RAF Lymington.

Amport House, west of Andover, was requisitioned in 1939 as the HQ of a maintenance command for Hampshire's airfields administering a whole range of specialist groups. RAF/army coordination took place at a requisitioned secondary school in Farnborough that was disbanded when work began to plan for D-Day in 1943. Farnborough Court then became the focus of RAF/army coordination. There is a larger debate about the effectiveness of the bombing campaign masterminded by Air Marshal Harris, but undoubtedly the role of Hampshire's airfields in the bombing was an important one. What must be recognized is the complex infrastructure that operated through the Air Ministry which enabled the building of airfields capable of supporting such a campaign. At its peak in 1944 when the United States Army Air Force (USAAF) presence was at its peak immediately prior to D-Day, 136 contractors were involved employing more than 50,000 men. From 1935 a whole design and development culture began to create barrack buildings, hangars and their annexes, armouries, stores, workshops and bomb storage areas. When new airfields were opened it became apparent that grass runways were not suitable for the heavy bombers being developed by the Allies and so major construction work was required to provide safe landing and take-off facilities using asphalt. By February 1940 a suitable airfield for bombers was required to have three strips: one of 1,400 yards and two of 1,000 yards. Special runways for crash landings meant a large amount of civil engineering because they had to be five times the length of a normal runway. For instance, at one airfield this work extended over 600 acres with 70 miles of drains and ducts and 1 million cubic yards of excavation.

Eisenhower on a visit to Stoney Cross airfield.

Air-crew at Ibsley.

[Source: CG]

Barbadian air-crew flying from Hampshire airfields. Many of these men lost their lives.

The effectiveness of the work that went into the design of these airfields is that at Odiham and Middle Wallop they can still be seen today. Some of the buildings reflect a shortage of timber so they were built of a combination of concrete and corrugated sheeting developed by Colonel P. Nissen, designer of the Nissen hut.

Three civilian airfields already in existence were taken over at Christchurch, Portsmouth and Eastleigh. New airfields were built at Hurn, Ibsley, Stoney Cross, Holmsley South, Thruxton, Lasham and Blackbushe. Construction took place in an atmosphere of crisis with the emphasis on utility producing a style of temporary brick. At Hartley Wintney a wooden manor house was pressed into service as a transit hotel for Blackbushe airfield. Lee-on-Solent, because of its naval link, had a control tower in 1942 that illustrated its naval influences, while Worthy Down boasted a tower resembling a water tower.

The vital building of hangars featured a number of designs but that most widely used featured doors at either end, was 250ft in length and had a height of 25ft. As larger aircraft were produced so the size of hangars had to increase such as the 'C' type still to be seen at Middle Wallop having a length of 300ft and a span of 150ft. These were built of metal and to save on materials were built to the same prototype. The expansion of airfields meant that between 1938 and 1940 transportable hangars were constructed with a 95ft span and a length of 150ft. They were known as the blister hangar which became the most familiar on Hampshire's airfields. Because of its cheapness it led to more than 300 of them being produced. At the permanent bases such as Stoney Cross and Ibsley there was accommodation of a high standard including catering for sick quarters and married and single men's accommodation.

Perhaps the most notable feature of the wartime airfield was the control tower. It represented a switch in airfield management with pre-1939 pilots simply being required to log in with the duty officer at the airfield. This altered dramatically with the creation of a special room or office monitoring and controlling operations on the airfield. However, by 1940 reports were being received by the Air Ministry that the runways of the county's airfields were brightly illuminated by moonlight. Work immediately commenced to turn them green. After Dunkirk, when invasion was considered likely, great efforts were put into plans to defend Hampshire's airfields. As late as 1942 there was a fear of attack on the airfields by paratroopers and the best means of defence against this was seen as planting explosives under runways to blow them up, thereby denying their use to the invader. The pipe mine system devised was carried out at Odiham, Blackbushe and Farnborough.

In the period before the declaration of war the government was in contact with large construction companies such as John Laing about the availability of their manpower and equipment resources. Some of these contractors had been building military projects since the mid-1930s for the War Ministry and had gauged from this the inevitability of approaching conflict. Laing reported that they had 4,000 men available, 21 horse-drawn vehicles, 12 cranes, 29 pumps, 75 concrete mixers, 11 lorries and 6 new Bedfords with trailers. Almost all the contractors working with the government were prepared to make teams available in emergencies. The final phase of airfield development was the advanced landing grounds built for fighter-bombers. These required a minimum of 1,000ft of runway and as part of second-front planning these should be within a 100-mile radius of Caen. There were eleven sites in Hampshire with three on the Isle of Wight. Eventually five sites were selected, with those being intended for use only in the period leading up to D-Day having minimal facilities. Pylewell, Bisterne, Winkton and Lymington were built around existing buildings. Needs Ore and Park Farm were examples of virgin fields that were pressed into service with tented accommodation for air-crew. Southwick House, where major strategic planning took place, boasted its own landing strip for senior military officers.

The bare bones of construction and location fail to tell the full story of these airfields. Chilbolton, situated on a plateau in the middle of Hampshire, played an important part in the aviation history of the war. Work began on its construction in 1938 and as already described it played an important role in supporting the activities of Fighter Command at nearby Middle Wallop. In 1941 work began to upgrade the airfield with the construction of a tarmac track. Accommodation for 2,800 staff was constructed and in 1943 American aircraft began to be based at Chilbolton. The P-47s were used for softening-up operations in the period prior to D-Day. After D-Day residents enjoyed a period of calm until Douglas C-47s arrived bringing back the wounded. The airfield was selected for airborne landings via gliders in 1944 at Arnhem in Operation MARKET GARDEN (the Battle of Arnhem). By 1945 a whole host of planes such as Mustangs, Typhoons and Martinets were using the airfield. It then went on to play an important role in the development of jet aircraft.

Winkton Airfield had similar origins, being located in deeply rural Hampshire and being associated with pubs like the Lamb Inn at Holfleet on the eastern edge of Winkton Village, the Carpenters Arms, the Crown and Three Tuns at Bransgore and the Woolpack in Sopley. The ones most popular with American airmen when they arrived were the Lamb Inn and the Woolpack. The Woolpack also doubled as a canteen. The majority of the airfield was in Sopley Village on land originally owned by Sopley Farm. Philip John Witt remembers the RAF Regiment putting up Nissen huts that had to be their base while the runways were under construction. The vicar of Sopley was Canon Charles Kirkham who was officiating chaplain for the RAF in both Sopley and Winkton. In 1943 development of the airfield built on a burial mound of the bodies of the fallen from one of King Alfred's battles with the invading Danes took place, despite the objections of Canon Kirkham. One of the air-crew located in tents remembers a group invading his tent in search of rabbit burrows, finding one and smoking out a rabbit which made a rabbit stew. Residents report frequent crashes and one Hurricane crashing and narrowly missing a major fuel site in 1943. Two aircraft crashed near Priests Lane in Sopley and the Home Guard seeking to rescue one of the air-crew struggled for some time to get him out because he was well over 6ft tall. The aircraft still had its bombs on board, which subsequently exploded. A place called New Barn was used as a theatre for entertainment for the Americans. The audience sat on 5-gallon fuel cans watching a stage consisting of two large shells 2ft 6in tall. The audience would beat tin cans instead of applauding. The Americans generously invited people from the surrounding area into their canteen where they saw types of food unknown since the advent of rationing. Bombs for bombers were brought up from Christchurch railway junction and stored in a sunken road that ran along the north-south runway. Use was made of matting laid by two Jeeps pushing rolls of it in front of them. Doug Nelmes, a tanker driver, described what it was like when a bomb exploded near his truck, blowing its hood off but not fracturing any of the tanks. Michael Dowding described returning planes flying in formation coming in to land at the airfield and peeling off to land and seeing the Thunderbolts taxiing up to land in the sunlight.

Stoney Cross opened in November 1942 to serve the RAF and the USAAF Ninth Air Force. It had one runway, two secondary runways and 'frying pan' dispersal pads with loops connecting to a perimeter track. Construction work was still going on when RAF Fighter Command, including P-51 Mustangs, arrived in January 1943 and 26 Squadron also arrived. No. 297 Squadron arrived in early March 1944 but the USAAF Ninth Air Force moved out together with the RAF in March 1944. Stoney Cross was known as USAAF Station AAF-452 for security reasons. Fighter aircraft based at Stoney Cross added to the Allied push for D-Day from 9 May 1944 by attacking railways, bridges and hangars in western France and providing escort for bombers targeting airfields and marshalling yards in strategically-important areas of France. The group involved the 367 Fighter Group which was then switched to direct support for the First Army on the ground in France. They were later moved on 6 July to Ibsley to allow the 387 Fighter Group to take their place at Stoney Cross. When the Americans moved to France the airfield became a major transport hub servicing not only Europe but the Far East and finally being released back to its owners in 1948.

RAF Andover was important for providing RAF maintenance and training as well as hosting two American fighter units. It also played a role previously mentioned during the Battle of Britain as a decoy site at Hurstbourne Tarrant. Andover itself was attacked twice in 1941 by German bombers believing it was a major airfield for Allied bombers. However, by February 1944 Andover was again being used as a base for the 401, 402 and 485 Fighter Squadrons of the 367 Fighter Group of the USAAF. Out of Andover they dive-bombed radar installations and flak towers and provided escort for bombers attacking vital areas prior to D-Day. After D-Day they moved on to the advanced landing ground at Cardonville in France. The USAAF lost thirty-one P-38s prior to the move to France. Between 9 December 1944 and 5 March 1945 the Canadian Army Air Observation Force was based at Andover equipped with Auster Mk 4 and 5 aircraft. The airfield became the centre for training Canadian and Commonwealth flight crews which included training to fly helicopters.

Holmsley, built at a cost of £588,042, was opened in October 1942 and provided a base for RAF Transport Command, Coastal Command and the American Air Force. Holmsley had the standard three-runway configuration with dispersal sites and accommodation occupying a wide area. Jack Phillips, who was based at Holmsley, recalled being met by one of the WAAF drivers when he left the train at Hinton Admiral Halt who was to take him to Holmsley South, his first station. He was a member of the Royal Canadian Air Force in the 418 City of Edmondson Squadron, joining a base that consisted mainly of Canadians but also some RAF navigators. They were designated as a night intruder squadron and were flying Mk 6 Mosquitos equipped with four 20mm cannon and four Browning machine guns and capable of carrying two 500lb bombs. He described Holmsley as being a friendly place where after tented accommodation he enjoyed smart Nissen huts, real beds, proper mattresses and a stove to provide effective heat. His only sad memory is watching helplessly as his best friend was shot down.

In among the physical details of Hampshire's airfields, the human cost in the lives of fighter and bomber crews must be remembered. The *Aldershot News* carried a short paragraph about a rear gunner desperate to take part in RAF attacks on Germany volunteering to be an extra gunner. He had never flown before but did not return from this attack on Berlin. By 1942 the same paper reported that the WAAF had become the largest women's service with all its number being volunteers. It had been founded in June 1939 when its members became involved in crucial cypher work. During 1940 WAAF members were awarded medals following German attacks on naval bases and airfields. They became recognized as an integral part of the RAF and took over the management of barrage balloon sites. They were now employed at fifty-one different sites acting as armourers and electricians. Reviewing the year, the *Aldershot News* claimed 1,358 German aircraft for the loss of 558 Allied aircraft. By 1943 the paper was reporting that £200,000 had been raised towards the purchase of four Lancaster bombers designed to make attacks on Germany's industrial heartland. Aldershot's squadron of its Air Training Corps produced a display of their work in Aldershot's High Street on 21 January 1941. Reports were coming back of local men who had gone to Canada to train as air-crew. Comments were made about how well heated the facilities were (clearly a comparison with the state of accommodation for Canadians in Britain), and how efficient the Canadians were in keeping engines operating in freezing conditions. The paper marked the acquisition of wings for Sergeant H.A. Wiles from Canada after being in Aldershot's Auxiliary Territorial Service (ATS) and joining the RAF a year earlier. It also reported that his brother was in a prisoner-of-war camp in Italy after being captured in Tunisia. Hampshire's young men completing their training in Canada were Sergeant W. Foster from Southampton, Sergeant P.L. Edwards from Fleet and L.J. Tought from Portsmouth. In December 1943 an RAF pilot from Fleet, Pilot Officer J.G. Barker, was reported to have won the DFC.

With optimism associated with indications that the aerial attacks had decreased came recognition of the heroism that had made it possible. The Rt Hon. Oliver Lyttelton, speaking as part of Aldershot's 'Wings for Victory' campaign featuring a procession through Aldershot on 25 May 1943, spoke of how his two previous speeches had been at a time when the country was in peril and now on the third occasion it was Germany that was in danger. The parade included representatives from RAF Bomber Command, the Air Training Corps, the 2nd Hampshire Home Guard, the Auxiliary Territorial

Training Corps, the Women's Royal Naval Service and the Women's Land Army. Music was provided by the Royal Army Service Corps and the Canadian Army Band.

The various fund-raising activities in Hampshire to raise money for the armed forces almost had a life of their own and became part of the war culture. This might be encapsulated in the story of the Alton Spitfire. There are two plaques in Alton Town Hall, one dating from October 1940 when money was raised for a Spitfire and the other from 1942 when money was sought for a warship. These savings movements were inspired by those of the Great War and as early as November 1939 a war savings movement sprung into life, which by 1943 claimed 300,000 street groups actively fund-raising for military activity and being supported by the BBC, films and posters. Objectively the result might have been to raise civilian morale rather than achieve the savings sought. Hampshire's campaign was launched following an appeal by Dr H.M. King in the *Hampshire Chronicle* of 27 July 1940. The first appeal was for a Hampshire Agricultural Fighter Plane (otherwise known as a New Forest Spitfire). This was followed by an appeal from Winchester for a fighter plane, an appeal from Portsmouth for two, succeeded by Gosport and the New Forest, Bournemouth, Southampton and Eastleigh. On the anniversary of the outbreak of war a Spitfire fund was launched in Alton and Rural Districts. It quickly reached its target amount but so quickly that the announcement of its success undermined a concert arranged for the Coldstream Guards when only £9.00 was raised by the concert. However, other fund-raising activities were far more successful and on 12 November a cheque was handed to Lord Beaverbrook for a Spitfire to be named the Alton and District Spitfire. The appeal for money in Winchester was not nearly so successful as in other parts of Hampshire, possibly due to comments that fund-raising should be aimed towards helping families who had suffered losses in the Battle of Britain.

In fact, identifying a particular Spitfire as that of Alton or anywhere else was difficult as they were rolling off the production line without any particular identification. Alton's donation of £5,520 was presented on 14 March 1941 and allocated to 266 Squadron with planes flown by pilots from Rhodesia who were operating out of Wittering. On 3 July 1942 the plane piloted by Sergeant R.J. Thorburn was shot down and the wounded pilot became a prisoner of war in Stalag 357 in Germany. Another Spitfire donated by Andover, the Andoverian, flew with 118 Squadron at Ibsley and survived the war. The Cat donated by Aldershot was on active service for six months before being used for training. Bournemouth's donated Spitfire survived the war but Winchester's plane assigned to 92 Squadron failed to return from an operation on 27 August 1941 and was posted as missing. The Mk 5 donated by the New Forest crashed as a result of a mid-air collision just three months after its maiden flight.

To mark these community-donated aircraft, illuminated manuscripts were presented to all savings committees for display in town halls and one can be seen in Alton Town Hall as well as in other Hampshire towns. A Certificate of Honour for the 1943 Wings for Victory campaign was given to the Alton and District Savings Committee and is in their Curtis Museum. Alton continued to appeal for support for the air war and accumulated savings of £240,000 by 10 April, enough to purchase five Lancaster bombers. Such enthusiasm was further kindled by the Dam Buster raid (Operation CHASTISE) and direct appeals locally by Squadron Leader Learoyd VC and Alton's MP. Learoyd's speech described the way in which donated bombers were sweeping the Channel and occupied Europe, bombing docks, factories and marshalling yards as well as providing protection for convoys. Publicity around the loss of Alton's Spitfire encouraged revenge through purchasing Lancaster bombers. The reality was that in 1943 these planes had a life expectancy of just three weeks, with Bomber Command losing 243 planes through operations, ninety-three of them being Lancasters.

Ibsley, straddling the forest boundary, was one of the New Forest's airfields that came to play an important role in the Second World War. The airfield took in the hamlet of Rockford and the village of Ellingham, being recognized as Blashford Lakes. Ibsley was built in the early stages of the war and opened in February 1941, having a short operational life until 1945. Construction took six months, coinciding with the heavy bombing of Southampton; rubble from bombed Southampton buildings was used in its construction during 1940–41. There were three tarmac runways, the main one being 4,800ft long, the second 4,200ft and the third 4,050ft. The buildings consisted of twelve blister hangars, fourteen aircraft pens and a concrete tower. No. 32 Squadron of Hurricane fighters was using Ibsley before its construction had finished. The one and only attack on Ibsley occurred at this time with little damage and no loss of life. Ibsley was immortalized in 1942 when David Niven starred in the film *The First of the Few* (renamed *Spitfire* in the United States), which was shot between operation sorties at Ibsley. Flying with 605 Squadron, Wing Commander 'Bunny' Currant claimed thirteen kills in the Battle of Britain operating from the airfield. For a short period after June 1942 the US Air Force operated out of Ibsley before returning it to the RAF in December 1942. Immediately prior to D-Day the USAAF returned with P-37 Thunderbirds and P-38 Lightnings until they followed the Allies to French and Belgian airfields. Spitfires based here were given the task of escorting Churchill and the king when they flew back from the January Conference in North Africa in 1943.

One of the American crewmen describes leaving Louisiana on 28 March 1944. Following his arrival in Portsmouth he went for training and twenty-one hours' flying time before being allocated to the 48 Fighter Group at Ibsley. Original hopes of staying at the manor house there were thwarted and he had to settle for life in one of the Nissen huts. After his first mission on 23 May 1944 he flew on fourteen different escort missions with bombers, each of three to four hours' duration. At this stage of the war he was dive-bombing and strafing bridges, railways yards and German troop concentrations and stores.

RAF Beaulieu was located next to the New Forest village of East Boldre, about 2 miles west of the village of Beaulieu and 5 miles from Lymington. It was opened on 8 August 1942 and was host to 311 Squadron of Czech fliers. It was both a bomber and fighter airfield providing a base for the USAAF from 1943. It had three asphalt runways. Further west at Christchurch, vital work on radar was taking place at the Air Defence Research and Development Establishment (ADRDE). A Bellman hangar was erected in 1940 which received aircraft from the Fleet Air Arm, HMS *Raven*, for its experimental work. Three more hangars were built between 1941 and late 1943 when the airfield was taken over by the Signals Research and Development Establishment. From 24 March to 8 April runways of steel mesh were laid by American engineers who also built shooting-in butts and bomb storage areas. The USAAF took total control of the airfield in March 1944 when squadrons equipped with Thunderbolts moved in. After D-Day they moved out and the RAF once again took control.

Lymington airfield was the location of the USAAF 50th Fighter Group. Work took place to prepare it as a fighter base with the USAAF arriving at the airfield on 16 April 1943. P-47 Thunderbolts were considered to be serviceable planes able to carry heavy loads. However, ground crews complained how difficult it was to start their engines in cold weather. Air-crews were housed in seven-man tents. In the days leading up to D-Day, strafing attacks were made on key areas such as Arras and known airfields and on 6 July planes were in action from Lymington covering the landing beaches. Hurn, 3 miles from Bournemouth, was a satellite for Ibsley. It was the base for special agents flying out in Lysander Mk 3 aircraft. It was also used as a base for Dakotas that transported 2,400 troops to North Africa. In 1944 rockets were attached to the Typhoons, and Mosquitos were brought in to interfere with the observation of D-Day by German radar.

Hartford Bridge, which has now become Blackbushe Aerodrome, came to play an important role in the war from 1943 when it underwent major development. In August experimental work with gliders had begun with staff from the RAE. Serious building work by Robert McAlpine began in 1942. In 1943 it was designated as a Bomber Command diversion centre. By December 1943 more than 3,000 personnel were based at Hartford Bridge. The wings based at the airfield were organized on a self-sufficient basis in preparation for a move into Europe. In preparation for D-Day it was a centre for producing accurate maps of the topography that the Allies were to encounter, particularly on the landing beaches and their environs. Spitfires and Mosquitos were fitted with cameras to enable accurate photos to be taken of the German support systems around the landing beaches, gun positions and airfields. On D-Day squadrons based at Hartford Bridge laid smoke on the landing beaches. Free French and Dutch squadrons also were involved in D-Day attacks. The cosmopolitan airfield enjoyed hospitality from Farnborough, Yateley and Owlsmoor as the whole airfield was mobilized on D-Day. Warrant Officer Weaver worked with eight French resistance fighters who had to be airlifted from France. The first squadron to fly from Hartford Bridge flew Tomahawks and Mustangs. After D-Day 137 Squadron concentrated on targeting German movement of troops and supplies in northern France. An incident at the airfield in the summer of 1941 illustrates the danger of working with aircraft movement on such a scale piloted by a whole range of nationalities. A Free French pilot in a Mustang paid the resident 342 Lorraine Squadron a visit. To mark his departure he made a low-level pass of the airfield. Unfortunately his propeller touched fuel pipes and cartwheeled across the airfield, disintegrating as it went and holing several planes in its path. An unfortunate French maintenance worker on a bicycle was caught up in this chaos and killed instantly. The only part of the plane intact was the cockpit, from which the French pilot stepped virtually unscathed.

CHAPTER FIFTEEN

Maple Leaves, Yanks and Kiwis

Maple Leaves

In many ways the fate of the Canadian forces in Hampshire provides an interesting bellwether for the course of the war. When volunteers were sought in Canada to fight in Europe, some 50,000 came forward, carrying on a traditional link between Aldershot and Canada that had seen Canadian troops appearing at the Aldershot Tattoo in 1932. The first group left Halifax, Nova Scotia on 10 December 1939. Thousands of people greeted them on their arrival in Scotland and twenty-four hours later they were in Aldershot, Hampshire. Their arrival coincided with the coldest winter since 1894 and they were in for a cold, dispiriting time of it. Heating in the barracks left by the 1st and 2nd British Expeditionary Force was minimal. They occupied the Wellington, Stanhope and Marlborough Lines but there was a shortage of arms for their training in the Caesars Camp area and civilian cars were used to transport the few guns that were available. On 8 June 1940 the king came to inspect them together with their Prime Minister, the Rt Hon. Mackenzie King. The French Canadian Regiment, the last to reach England, provided the guard of honour. The prime minister brought a message from Canada for the assembled officers and men, stating that far from being forgotten they were uppermost in the thoughts of those in Canada. He alluded to the impatience in the Canadian ranks regarding the lack of action following the decision not to send Canadian troops to Norway in April. There was similar frustration when the decision was made not to send the Canadians to the besieged Dunkirk.

However, the war came to them when nine HE bombs were dropped on Guillemot Barracks and Wellington Barracks on 6 July, killing seven, and on the nearby parade ground, killing three and wounding another thirty. Some attempt was made to compensate the Canadians through functions at Aldershot's Dominion Club and dances every night at the local palais de dance in Aldershot's Queens Road, St Augustine in Hale, the Rechabite Hall, Ash Road and the RAE Assembly Rooms with Don Wagstaffe's Band, the Rug Cutters and Ray Ellington's band. In all, five cinemas were in operation in Aldershot. Local entrepreneur Bob Potter organized three bands that played every night at dance halls in the area. Out of these events, some permanent relationships developed leading to marriages and local girls subsequently travelling to Canada.

With British forces in deep trouble at Dunkirk, a Canadian force was hastily landed at Brest but events overtook them and with the fall of Paris they were hastily withdrawn. In essence, with the BEF in total disarray, the Canadians represented, with the small New Zealand Regiment, the only coherent force capable of defending the country. On 1 October the Canadians were transferred to Sussex and planning began for the raid on Dieppe. The Canadian tunnellers were called to Gibraltar to construct barracks on the Rock and another group was sent to Spitsbergen, northern Norway, as a preventative measure against attacks on Allied convoys. Canadian medics arrived and busied themselves setting up a fifty-bed hospital. In March 1942 Canadian troops participated in the St Nazaire raid. By summer 1942 there were 200,000 Canadian troops in Britain. During the summer, planning for an attack on Dieppe was taking place at Crondall, close to Aldershot. Observers were shocked by the almost total disregard for security as the troops assembling for the raid spoke not only of the raid but also its destination. Again some commentators refer to what happened to the Canadians as being little short of murder, with 907 of them dead following the raid of 19 August, 1,864 captured and a further 508 wounded. The only redeeming feature was that Jack Nissenthall, carrying out vital work in radar, was able to gain access to the German radar system and through this devise ways of blocking German radar which proved crucial for D-Day. This was the Canadians' first brush with military action and the limits of their training were apparent. In the days following the raid, ambulances carrying Canadian wounded stretched from Farnborough clock tower to the Cambridge Military Hospital. Stretchers lay for the whole half-mile of the Cambridge Hospital corridor. The Princess Patricia Canadian Light Infantry played an active role in the invasion of Sicily and the Canadians won their first two VCs during the Allied campaign in Italy. Of the 92,000 fighting there, 6,700 were killed. During 1943, as planning for D-Day was stepped up, training for landings took place in Studland Bay. The important role of Canada was highlighted by the Allies holding their conference in Quebec, during which Churchill paid tribute to the role being played by Canadian soldiers.

As D-Day approached, Canadian airmen were very busy at Blackbushe with the airfield becoming so busy that some aircraft were forced to land on the A30. Real problems were developing with heavy vehicles literally chewing up the tarmac surfaces of roads from north Hampshire to the departure areas for the invasion force. As D-Day approached, Canadian forces were part of the columns of military vehicles packing the whole of Queen's Avenue. As in the First World War, the parade grounds were packed with troops destined for France. The air was full of the drone of Dakotas, while bored Canadian troops waiting for the order to move occupied themselves playing crown and anchor (a dice game). This was a force of 3.5 million of which 150,000 landed on D-Day. There were 11,500 planes involved and 3,500 gliders as well as a merchant and auxiliary fleet of 1,500 plus 4,000 landing craft and 1,213 warships. Towards the end of May, in order to achieve secrecy, the Canadian camps were sealed off prior to the Canadians destined to be part of the landings on JUNO beach moving to Portsmouth and Southampton. For the Canadians May 1944 was hectic with desperate efforts to tighten the screws for the invasion plan. There were days of waiting confined to camps so that the go-ahead to be ordered by Eisenhower from his headquarters in Southwick fitted within a period between 5 and 10 June when the tides at Normandy would be right. Although Canadian troops had not been told that they were destined to land in France, in the prevailing atmosphere it was clear that something much more than an exercise was about to take place. If we follow Bombardier Ted Dyke from D Troop, 66th Battery, 14th Field Regiment, Royal Canadian Artillery from 4 June moving from his camp to the south coast we will find him embarked at sea on 5 June frustrated because of the bad weather causing a delay until the following day. The men had waited in Britain for two and a half years for the move towards the Normandy beaches which now appeared before them at 2.00 am on 6 June. JUNO, their landing beach, was between the two British beaches of GOLD and SWORD. Ted Dyke shared his landing craft with commandos and engineers, the first to land. As they approached the beach they came under heavy fire from machine guns and mortar and 100 yards from the shore the rear of their landing craft was blown off its mother ship by a small mine attached to a post, part of the beach defences. Relieved that his feet could touch the bottom but in water up to his shoulders, he held his Sten gun above his head and began to walk towards the beach. Shortly after 7.00 am Ted was one of the first Canadians to set foot in France. Once on the beach he successfully raced the 150 yards to the sea wall. Later in the morning he achieved his objective of setting up an observation post capable of directing the guns of ships out at sea onto specific German targets. There then followed the main thrust of Canadian troops with a message 'Good Luck Canada' being transmitted by semaphore. Despite encountering many hazards, by the end of 6 June the Canadians had achieved most of their objectives. However, many hard battles lay ahead such as that of the 1st Canadian Parachute Regiment which was the first Canadian unit to cross the Rhine. On 6 May 1945 Ted Dyke went behind enemy lines to accept the surrender of the German command at Emden and noted the overwhelming sense of sadness among the German troops. At the command post in Emden the war ended with the Canadians having their largest force in history with a general, twelve divisions and four independent brigades. A total of 12,579 Canadians had given their lives in order to free Europe.

Hitler's retaliation came in the form of the V-1 flying bomb known as the doodlebug or buzz-bomb, a missile with great explosive power, and his target was southern England. One V-1 struck in Aldershot showering glass on the girls in a nearby girls' school and killing a girl in the class. Evidence that the war was still capable of exerting its deadly visitation came when on 11 August 1944 there was a direct hit on Runfold, killing a farmer, his wife and daughter and injuring others in the vicinity.

In the meantime, after some months of hosting the Canadians, Aldershot and its surrounding towns had to grow accustomed to their visitors. One notable feature vis-a-vis their hosts was how well-paid they were. They could go on leave with the then princely sum of £1 in their pocket, while their British counterparts had to exist on much less. They had a plentiful supply of cheap Caporal cigarettes, cheaper than the British Players brand, and were ready to trade their food parcels and other possessions. They were less vigorously disciplined than their British counterparts who were expected to be at attention, even when having a casual conversation with an officer. The Canadians were attractive to local women and because of this there was resentment from the local male population, a resentment that was also evident when the American forces arrived. This was offset to some extent by the generosity shown to their community through commanding officers turning a blind eye to food and clothing being taken out of the camps as gifts to local families. Great effort was put into organizing Christmas parties with children being bussed into Canadian venues. However, there was some resentment on the Canadians' part about being fleeced by local shopkeepers, possibly because of their lack of understanding of sterling currency. There was heavy drinking with the Canadian Military Police developing a direct method of dealing with drunks by coshing them over the head and returning the unconscious men to their barracks. One local policeman intervened at a fish and chip shop in Cove, only to leave through its front window. Perhaps the reality of the relationship between the Brits and the Canadians may be found in a letter received by the Canadian High Commissioner. The writer stated that both she and her daughter had been in a relationship with the same Canadian soldier: 'As a result both my daughter and I are pregnant. Not that I hold this against your soldier but the last time he was here he took my daughter's bicycle which she needs to get to work. Can you get him to return it?'

Canadian troops participated fully in the celebration of the end of the war on 6 July 1945. A grand military parade was organized at Aldershot's recreation ground and 10,000 local people attended. In the flag-draped recreation ground the Canadian army bands could be heard playing. Thunderbolt flashes were let off by the Home Guard. The largest party took place in Aldershot's Haig Road where trestle tables strained under the weight of jam tarts, jellies and sandwiches, as well as Lily's famous blancmange. At the RAE, Canadian troops were very much in evidence among the 500 who packed the RAE Assembly Hall for the victory dance. The years of not being able to mark Guy Fawkes' night were swept away by the lighting of bonfires all over the town and in Cove and Farnborough. During the war 1,859 premises had been damaged, with the council patching up most of them.

However, in the following weeks there was something of a hangover from the VE Day celebrations. Canadian troops brought back from Europe were anxious to get home and the preparation for repatriation seemed to crawl along at a ridiculously slow pace in the centres where the men were housed. There was the dull routine of barrack life after three years in action, tending to produce idleness and boredom. Young soldiers had little to do but sit in camp waiting for their shipping to be arranged. The loss of so many ships meant that available berths were extremely limited. Priority was being given to the war in the east that still continued. A growing resentment developed towards local traders in Aldershot who many Canadians regarded as cheating them. Problems arose with delayed pay and in a Europe of severe food shortages, rationing was severe. As early as June 1945 there had been a rise in arrests and convictions of Canadian soldiers for petty offences but on 21 June four teenage Canadian soldiers were convicted of stealing a taxi and robbing the driver. On 4 July at 10.15 am a group of protesting Canadians assembled at the bottom of Hospital Hill in Aldershot making demands for the immediate release of Canadians in jail. When they reached the cells at the police station they were convinced that no Canadians were being held there, despite being informed to the contrary by Private L.A. States, a member of the Pioneer Corps, who appeared to be something of an exhibitionist. The group rapidly grew to 500 before moving into Aldershot to smash 90 windows and badly damage 25 shops. On the following night considerable damage was done to Aldershot Arcade but the worst hit area was Union Street. Nothing was spared, with even the Red Cross centre being attacked. Wellington Street presented a bizarre sight with tailors' dummies stripped of their clothes lying in the street. Clearly the riot caught both police and the army authorities unprepared and a Canadian vehicle with a loudspeaker over which a Canadian officer was seeking to restore order was violently rocked by the rioters. When the latter finally dispersed, £15,000 worth of damage had been done and 200 shops had been attacked after two nights of rioting. Extra Canadian Military Police were brought in from outlying barracks and Canadian officers patrolled the streets using loudspeaker vans. The Military Police objective was to force the rioters out of the town centre rather than make arrests. General Montague, Chief of the General Forces, expressed his anger and shame at what had happened and delegated British soldiers for a general clean-up in Aldershot. Canadian troops were hurriedly moved away from Aldershot to other camps with the Canadians' *Maple Leaf* newspaper referring to the rioters as 'a motley group of hoodlums'. As a result of the riot, 22,000 sq ft of glass lay on the streets of the town. The Canadian government paid £15,000 towards restoration. Courts martial took place with the five ringleaders being sentenced to periods in prison ranging from sixteen months to seven years.

Three years after the disaster of Dieppe on 19 August 1942, a thanksgiving service was held at the recreation ground in Aldershot and the announcement was made that Aldershot Borough Council would confer the Freedom of the Borough on the Canadian Army Overseas. On 26 September, again at the recreation ground, a scroll of the Freedom of the Borough was handed to the Canadian General Montague. The general responded by thanking the people of the Hampshire and Surrey parts of the Aldershot Command Area for the hospitality that had been shown to Canadian troops since their arrival. Then it was out onto the streets of Aldershot with gleaming bayonets, beating drums and colours held aloft. This was in very sharp contrast to the riots just weeks before. Remembered too was the generous gift of a mobile canteen to Aldershot, consisting of an area capable of accommodating four or more assistants dispensing refreshments which became a welcome sight in wartime Aldershot.

Yanks

Most British people's concept of Americans was shaped by dominant Hollywood movies creating stereotypes from the silver screen enjoyed every week. J.B. Priestley, in his *English Journey* with its evocative portraits of Britain in the 1930s, talks of thousands of women made over in the image of their favourite screen goddess. From 1942, with the arrival of the GIs in Hampshire, it was a case of unpacking the stereotypes of the dream factory along with candy, Coca Cola and nylons. A member of one of the concert parties at the time recalled that after one of their shows at Stoney Cross base they jumped into the Americans' Jeeps and raced around the planes just as they were taking off. She said the Americans seemed to be a law unto themselves in comparison with British soldiers who were much more strait-laced. Like the Canadians, Roosevelt had sent his army to Britain enjoying a level of pay five times that of British soldiers. It should be remembered that the evacuation of poorer areas of Gosport, Southampton and Portsmouth had revealed levels of poverty that made the GIs appear as demi-gods of affluence able to shower undreamed-of gifts on those around them. A feature of life in the American bases around Hampshire was the parties regularly organized by the Americans, which women living in the surrounding areas were enticed to attend. Joyce Carlisle recalled going to a cinema in the Southampton area and seeing one of her husband's relatives snogging with a GI. A clear reflection of this was the many GI brides from Hampshire and the county's contribution to the 9,000 babies born out of wedlock. For the children of Hampshire who were virtually starved of sweets, there was a constant supply of bubble-gum and other confectionery that only the GIs were able to provide. These were distributed by men who shocked star-struck Hampshire with their ordinariness.

By the time the war was over, some 3 million GIs had passed through Britain, including 100,000 black American troops, a shock especially to rural Hampshire where a black face was extremely uncommon. When black American GI cooks arrived at the Boys' Technical School in Hilsea, their arrival caused a considerable stir in Cosham High Street. However, possibly because of the country's imperial inheritance there was not the level of racial intolerance that many of the GIs brought with them in their segregated regiments. Nevertheless, there were strong taboos about children being born out of wedlock. If the child was black, the taboo was even greater. What was it like to have a black GI dad? Pauline Natividad finally traced her father, a medic and a veteran of the OMAHA Beach landings, in later life and contact with him was life-enriching. Ruth Lange from Southampton received a free airline ticket for a tearful meeting with her GI father. Elizabeth Carpenter, living in Burley, reported how black GIs seemed to be given the worst jobs such as guarding the ammunition dump or vehicle-cleaning. Publicans in Hampshire noted a different attitude to money to their British customers with money simply being left on the counter before and after transactions. For many of Hampshire's GIs their 'special relationship' with this country was a particular town or place to which some returned after the war. For many young people denied 'edgy' music by the BBC, the GIs brought with them R&B (rhythm and blues), blues music and jazz. The Americans in Southampton marvelled at the sight of the first British queue and the stoic way in which women would wait for hours to obtain scarce foodstuffs.

When the 251 men of the USAAF 313 Fighter Squadron arrived in Lymington at 1.15 on the morning of 15 April 1942, they were not expecting that their accommodation at Winkton would be in tents but they should have been suspicious when they saw the mud on the boots of the advance party sent to meet them. Jude James, who had been through some of the worst of the bombing, was amazed to see how much smarter the American uniforms were than those of the British. Those who remember remark on how relationships with the Americans were so transitory because they went overseas and never returned. Esther Pring's fiancé was killed in France in the second week after D-Day. Ann Parnaby from Bournemouth recalled the Americans billeted in B&B places in Bournemouth and remembered one GI who had married at the age of 19 and after being drafted arrived in the UK. British families looked after men like that and in return received generous gifts from their rations. Marjorie Mathew of Lymington commended the American light-heartedness which alleviated some of the grimness of the war. The American troops arrived here without a provision to give them any support in the community in which they were going to live. This was provided by the Women's Voluntary Service that was responsible for opening up hundreds of homes to provide crucial support for US servicemen and women. An example of this was in Ringwood where forty US pilots at RAF Hurn were welcomed into local homes. As with the Canadians, nothing succeeded so well as the children's parties in Hampshire organized by US servicemen. Later the American military organized what they called 'flop houses' that provided rest for the battle-weary. These were sometimes available for men who had completed half a tour of duty. One of these was located in the Tudor manor house in Stockbridge. Another was situated in Alresford and in June 1944 at Growelle Court in Bournemouth, now the Heathlands Hotel.

The arrival of the American military in Britain from 1942 must have rather resembled the Norman Conquest, not only from their sheer numbers but how deeply they were embedded throughout all of Hampshire and into the culture of the county. Take their presence in Lymington, for instance, the principal town of the New Forest. Almost the whole gamut of military activity could be found in just one small town because of its strategic importance for D-Day. What stood out was the presence of the technical support units for the invasion plan and for the bombing campaign against Germany, such as the Mobile Reclamation and Repair Squadron, service groups, the Quartermaster Company, ordnance and supply companies and engineering companies. Surrounding the circumstances of D-Day, there was the Weather Squadron playing a vital role in the operation of aircraft over Europe. There were four Fighter Bombing Groups listed, together with the service groups necessary to support them as well as a special branch of the Military Police for aviation. The focus of activities around port installations was revealed in Southampton but also its role as a base for the 29th American Infantry. At Winkton the presence of the 404 Fighter Group and support for this group was highlighted, while Alresford hosted the 47th Infantry Regiment of the US army.

In 1943 the War Office purchased 2,106 acres of land at Barton Stacey 7 miles south-east of Andover, close to the A303 for communication. The land was intended for training purposes but in February 1944 it was the base for key elements of the US army such as the 3rd Army Group, the 9th Divisional Artillery, the 26th, 34th, 60th and 84th Field Artillery battalions, the 39th Infantry Regiment, the 70th Tank Regiment and the 741st Tank Battalion. Clearly because this was an area purposely designed to provide facilities for artillery and tank training, it was natural that there was a large-scale concentration of American troops here. The RAF had designated Andover for a key role in maintenance so the American military utilized this not only for aircraft but also for general military engineering with the 365 Group as well as fighter squadrons. At Andover from February to July 1944, Fighter Squadrons 401, 402 and 495 of the 370 Fighter Group of the USAAF were deployed in support of D-Day. Lockheed Lightning P-38 aircraft carried out bombing raids on the Cotentin Peninsula. Of these, thirty-eight were lost.

With the Americans came their hospital provision such as the 306th Station Hospital at Eastmoor, approximately 3 miles south-west of Ringwood on the Ringwood to Bournemouth Road which was ready to receive its first patients on 24 November 1943. Huts for its staff had concrete floors, asbestos board roofs and each had a coal-burning stove. Their accommodation left something to be desired because they were housed in 128 scattered buildings. It was considered that washing and bathing facilities were adequate, as were the messing facilities in the hospital. Although there were meant to be additional rations for patients above 'field rations', only 70 per cent of this was actually achieved. This hospital was required to provide emergency treatment for soldiers in the vicinity and discharge them within thirty days. On 16 January 1944 143 US Army Postal Unit arrived to base themselves at the hospital and provide postal services for the 306th and troops in the surrounding area. On 10 February four officers, six nurses and forty support staff arrived for training in preparation for D-Day. The 306th was involved in a large-scale training exercise on 21 and 22 February when at twelve hours' notice they accepted 284 patients. On 18 March the 306th ceased to operate as a hospital and its function became a tented reception centre operating near Tidworth.

In December 1943 a small group of American army officers, nurses and support staff moved into the Royal Victoria Hospital at Netley, near Southampton, to prepare for its takeover by American medical staff. A 15-acre vegetable garden was prepared for cultivation to support the new occupants of Netley. The land was overrun with rats but with the cooperation of Southampton's sanitary officer the problem was rectified. The absence of specimen bottles for diagnostic work was overcome via an appeal to the WVS who responded with a generous supply of jam jars and preserve bottles. Netley was identified as the hospital responsible for dealing with an expected influx of casualties following the D-Day landings and so became the 28th US General Hospital, with the western side of the site becoming the 110th US Army Hospital represented by a single-storey building. By February 1944 the main Netley building was occupied as the base hospital for the 12th US Navy. Some idea of the condition of Netley was given by a VAD who worked there prior to the American takeover and described it as a dump. After being called up she joined No. 4 Company based at Netley along with seventy other VADs from all walks of life and age groups including some who had served in the Great War and the latter proved to be real tyrants. The nurses' quarters were in old barrack rooms which were in such a state that a lot of work was required to make them habitable. Washing facilities and lavatories were outside and taking a bath required walking along a long corridor to a single bath without a plug. Clearly in December 1943 there was much work for the Americans to do. There seemed to be little disappointment when the keys for Netley were handed over to the group setting up the 28th US General Hospital. Alan Whitelock had been ordered to report to Netley on 17 July 1943. He noted its railway line leading directly from the docks and its antiquated state. At 1.00 am he was at Southampton Station unloading patients from the Middle East.

The Park Prewett Hospital, operated through American Hospitals in Britain Ltd, provides an interesting insight into how a hospital of this kind operated in the British context. It was 2 miles outside Basingstoke which at that time had a population of 7,000, swollen because it was accommodating evacuees from London. There were also troops from surrounding bases using the town's amenities. The hospital enjoyed a good transport link with Basingstoke. The Medical Director of American Hospitals in Britain in 1941, Dr Philip Wilson, described Park Prewett's brick construction, its double-decker wards and its shape like a large oval. It had open grass courts inside the oval which were connected by a concrete walkway. Their ward block had three double-decker buildings all close to each other and the hospital's X-ray department with the physiotherapy department occupied one of the top floors of the wards. The operating theatre was in a separate building between two of the wards. Clearly expecting an influx of wounded, the hospital offered 1,500 beds and had a large residential staff of surgeons and medical graduates. Staff at Park Prewett included five orthopaedic surgeons, a general surgeon, a plastic surgeon and an internist. Dr Wilson reported that nurses able to work in the operating theatre were being recruited but as there were not enough American nurses available to cover all the American hospital wards, one ward was being singled out for the genuine American nursing experience. In March 1941, when Dr Wilson drafted his letter, the hospital was treating two-thirds military patients and one-third civilian. He mentioned that there were still patients being treated after Dunkirk, together with those injured as the result of bombing in Hampshire. There were difficulties in finding adequate accommodation for medical staff because of the influx of evacuees from London.

Dr Wilson described the work the hospital was doing with patients from air-raids. Standard practice in the treatment of arm and leg injuries with severe fracturing was surgical cleansing under full anaesthetic, the use of a new chemical to sterilize the wound, the insertion of pins and the sealing off of the wound. These methods were a great improvement on those employed in the Great War and saved limbs that formerly would have been amputated. Treatment of this kind had originally been devised during the Spanish Civil War. He mentioned that this pioneering work aroused considerable interest among British surgeons and was to be influential in new methods of treatment as the war progressed.

Because the pioneer of plastic surgery, Sir Harold Gillies, lived near Basingstoke, the hospital's resident plastic surgeon was closely advised in this aspect of Park Prewett's work. They were receiving pilots who had been burned in their cockpits during and after the Battle of Britain. Major work in the reconstruction of these men's faces was carried out at the hospital.

Collection of photos from the American Hospital, Park Prewett, Basingstoke.

A cheerful GI in Hampshire.

At the American Hospital, Park Prewett, Basingstoke.

GIs in camp in Hampshire.

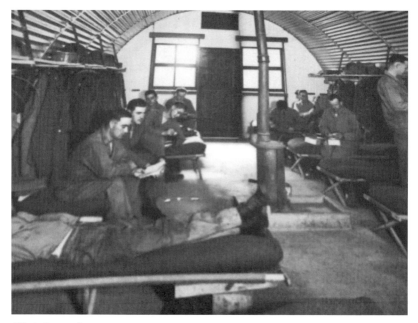

GIs in barracks.

Kiwis

New Zealand forces were involved in Hampshire's war effort right from
the beginning. The 2nd New Zealand Division of its Expeditionary Force
on its way to Egypt was diverted to the Aldershot Command organizing
home defence. General Bernard Freyberg was in command of a group of
men that included the Maori Battalion. The War Office gave him a choice of
Winchester with billets or Aldershot with tents and Aldershot was chosen. The
5th Brigade's war diary records this period as one of the happiest times spent
overseas. It turned out that the tents were not employed and they were billeted
with private families or in barns, oast houses and requisitioned buildings.
The importance of sport was illustrated by the report of a final rugby match
being played at Watchett's recreation ground in nearby Camberley. The New
Zealand HQ 5th Brigade was in Aldershot where there was specialist training
and drills. Following an inspection by HRH the Princess Royal at Mytchett, it
was agreed that they had reached a high level of efficiency. At Christmas 1940
50 per cent of the force was able to take leave, some enjoying the facilities
offered by Aldershot's Dominion Club as well as those offered in private
homes. For those remaining in camp there was consolation from the severe
weather in the form of parcels from New Zealand.

Later in the war the New Zealand nursing service established a unit at the Prince Connaught Hospital in Aldershot to assist New Zealand PoWs returning from Germany with serious health problems following their internment. New Zealand contributed 140,000 men and women to the Allied war effort. Many young New Zealanders who served in Hampshire in the army, RAF or Royal Navy had their lives changed completely. One such was John Maturin who arrived in Hampshire with the New Zealand Expeditionary Force. John went to Greece and Crete as part of those disastrous campaigns which, even at the age of over 90, would wake him in the middle of the night with nightmares. During his time in Aldershot he met Doris and at the end of the war came back and married her, settling in Frimley Green just across the Hampshire border. Rose Cullen from Cove married Private John Harbottle from the New Zealand Expeditionary Force on 14 December 1940 at St Christopher's Church in Cove. Harbottle's best man was Private Charles, also of the New Zealand force. Harbottle was captured by the Germans in North Africa and spent hard years in an Italian PoW camp. After the war, he and his wife moved to New Zealand.

The author has chosen Pilot Officer John Rundle as an example of the hundreds of New Zealand Air Force personnel in Hampshire. He was born in Christchurch and worked at the railway workshops at Addington before applying to join the New Zealand Air Force in February 1940. After training in Canada, on 28 December 1942 he was posted as a pilot officer. He then began training to fly bombers. On 18 February 1943 with a crew of British, Australian and New Zealanders in a Sterling bomber equipped with new drop magnetic bombs his plane was limping back to base after being severely damaged by anti-aircraft fire. Some 4 miles from Alton he realized that the plane was about to crash. He ordered the crew to abandon the plane. The last to leave, he was killed by the plane's propeller. John Rundle is buried in Brookwood Cemetery, Woking.

There was a New Zealand flight of Mustangs based at Eastleigh Airport and two of the planes in the flight collided and crashed in fields close to Portsmouth railway line. The grisly, macabre part of the story is that Ian Douglas swimming in the River Itchen found the head of one of the pilots in the reeds.

Arthur Clouston was a test pilot born in the north of the South Island of New Zealand and had been bitten by the flying bug. In the pre-war atmosphere of pioneering aviation journeys he paid to acquire a pilot's licence. After being told that there were no vacancies in the New Zealand Air Force he sold a prosperous car business and travelled to the UK seeking to enter the Royal Air Force. Unfortunately he failed his medical examination because of high blood pressure but fortunately he had a letter of introduction from Sir Keith Park, Wing Commander at RAF Headquarters, a fellow New Zealander, who managed to steer his application through successfully. Clouston served for four years with the RAF before becoming a civilian test pilot at RAE Farnborough in 1935 where he flew many developing models of planes. A highly-skilled flier, he had been part of the Hendon Air Display team who were seen as the Red Arrows of their day. At the outbreak of war he returned to the RAF as a squadron leader. However, he was frustrated that his test pilot role prevented him from playing an active role in combat so that when a Heinkel appeared in the Aldershot sky dropping bombs on the camp he took to the air in an unarmed Spitfire. When he used the only armed Spitfire at Farnborough to shoot down an Me 100 over the Channel, he celebrated with a victory roll over the airfield. Later in the war, Clouston distinguished himself as the squadron leader for 224 Squadron flying Liberators tracking German submarines in the Atlantic. In 1944 he was awarded the DSO.

A decorated New Zealand pilot.

CHAPTER SIXTEEN

Living Through It: Aldershot 1942–43

Moves began at the start of 1942 to recruit as many available women as possible towards the war effort. In Aldershot and other places campaigns began to recruit for the ATS. The organization had already proved invaluable in augmenting the work of the armed forces. Those recruited took over the clerical work often undertaken by men involving shorthand, typewriting, filing, tabulation, checking, duplication and book-keeping. A whole range of other duties were also learned such as draftsmanship, catering, tailoring and carrying out vital roles as messengers. Outdoor occupations included car, ambulance and lorry-driving, vehicle maintenance, searchlight operation, sound detector work, observation and fire-control. Those promoting the ATS emphasized the good pay it offered and the opportunity to learn a trade. Indeed, in some areas of Hampshire where in the 1930s the only opportunity open to a girl leaving school was to go into service, what was offered by the ATS for women between the ages 17 and 43 presented a new horizon. For women with husbands serving in the armed forces leave arrangements could be made that coincided with their husbands. The ATS offered twenty-four hours' leave every week and seven days' leave every three months. A special parade of those recruited was planned for 21 June through Aldershot supported by the band of the Royal Military School of Music, the march concluding in Princess Gardens.

Despite the success in recruitment for the ATS, the *Aldershot News* of 2 January reported a crisis in recruitment of labour and the need for at least a 25 per cent increase in volunteers coming forward. At the start of 1942, commenting on the previous year, there was criticism of the level of drunkenness in the town despite the community action in buying war bonds, the Spitfire fund, war weapons donations and the air-raid distress fund. Fund-raising for Warship Week in Aldershot commenced on 14 February, Valentine's Day, also the date of a notable naval victory in the Napoleonic Wars. The aim was to raise £175,000 towards a submarine HMS *Tuna* that went on to be the launch pad for the cockleshell heroes' attack on Bordeaux. The Commander-in-Chief of Portsmouth, Admiral Sir William James KGB, said Aldershot's bullet had travelled halfway to its target by raising £86,000. There

Spitfire Week in Andover.

was a parade of more than 1,000 army, navy and support services personnel through the beflagged streets in the army town under the heading 'The Navy's here'. Admiral James said how vital submarines of this kind were for the Battle of the Atlantic. The choice faced by the country was between sacrifice and slavery. By March £141,000 had been raised in Farnborough towards war weapons. Farnborough had adopted the corvette HMS *Shearwater*. In March, Captain Tasker, presenting a plaque marking Farnborough's donation, reminded his audience in Farnborough of the sacrifices made by the men of the navy and of the Merchant Navy in order to feed the country. One of the gunners on the *Shearwater* had shot down a German plane and had won the DSM.

The first of limited reports appeared in the *Aldershot News* about the hideous conditions in Dachau concentration camp in Germany. Comments were made about the food offered not being 'fit for pigs'. In April, thirteen of the shelters built by Aldershot Council were found to have major faults in construction and had to be demolished. Residents were advised to build their own shelters. However, an army minister, the Rt Hon. Ernest Browne MC MP, advised that the best way to conquer stress was to volunteer for duty in the war. This benevolence did not extend to the theatre because on 18 April thirty-five actors in Aldershot were prosecuted by the Lord Chancellor for alluding to 'fun in a back street', risqué ballet poses and using the word 'bloody' during a play at the Hippodrome. However, in June, as an indication of how pre-war political attitudes had changed, Aldershot donated £1,500 to the Anglo-Soviet Society for an X-ray machine for the Soviet Union.

'Getting by' meant learning how to make do with the food available through rationing. Even though what came out of a tin often appeared unappetizing, it could be made palatable with a little patience. As well as stewed steak and vegetables and shepherd's pie, there were suggestions for a whole range of gelatine and meat roll dishes that could be broken up and mixed with vegetables. *Aldershot News* readers were advised that on a dark winter's day adding mashed potatoes and carrots to a meat dish in this way could brighten the day. The menu then went on to suggest stuffed potatoes and to advise how these might be prepared. For those still fortunate enough to get hold of tinned salmon, advice was given as to how this might be prepared, as suggestion was also given for a fish rarebit. Throughout all these menu suggestions, there was advice on how to make use of all available materials, even down to not wasting stale bread.

Every member of Fleet Football Club who had just won the Aldershot Junior Cup was now serving in the army, navy, Air Force or civil defence. The *Aldershot News* was beginning to highlight numbers of its readership serving in the Middle East, Sicily and other British war zones. Appeals were made for money towards the defence of Stalingrad. In 1942 the global character of the war was marked by the suggestion of a 'United Nations Day' in Aldershot. (This preceded the foundation of the United Nations organization in 1945 but followed the 'Declaration of United Nations' by Franklin D. Roosevelt in January 1942.) The day coincided with ceremonies to mark the flag of the United States. The flags were out all through Aldershot as members of the fire and police services, civil defence personnel, St John's Ambulance and the Air Training Corps in their blue uniforms marched accompanied by the Royal Military College Band and bands from the Canadian army. Appeals were made to recognize the work being carried out by transport workers supported by a publication from the Ministry of Information which highlighted stories like that of the bus driver who, seeing a house on fire during a bombing raid, dashed inside and rescued seven people and then calmly recommenced his journey. His only concern at that time was to step on it to make up for lost time. There was also a salute to the lorry drivers who braved real danger to drive imported foodstuffs from the docks. As in the First World War, there was a great drive to provide food parcels to British PoWs and this became more acute with the fall of Singapore where the Japanese appeared to pay little heed to the Geneva Convention in terms of the basic rights of prisoners. British PoWs in Germany were in receipt of parcels from home far more regularly than those in the Far East.

The role of young people in the war effort was not neglected, with the formation of an Aldershot Girls' Training Corps consisting of a commandant, vice commandant, adjutant and company officer with four sections, each of twenty-five. These officers would need to be vetted by the education authority. Mass mobilization meant that some bad pennies were swept up as in the case of Harold Perkins from Farnborough, who was before the court for pocketing allowances that should have been paid to members of the local Home Guard in which he was an officer. Although Home Guard service was a voluntary activity, when long periods of guard duty were involved a subsistence allowance was paid. Total deficits amounted to over £200.

As with food, the war effort involved the rationing of fuel featured in Aldershot's Battle of Fuel campaign. An exhibition was staged by the Mid Southern Utility Company. Whereas the gas industry had extolled the virtues of the consumption of manufactured fuel, there must now be a concerted effort to economize with its use. In the case of coal, the saving of 2lb per day per household would produce a saving of 2 million tons of national consumption. Half a ton of coal was required to produce the steel for a 9in shell and for a 25-pounder gun 5 tons of coal were required. Speaking to a fuel-saving conference, Fred Ryman from the Merchant Navy described how many colliers were vulnerable to bombing and whereas he made fifty trips before the war, that was now reduced by half due to the necessity of waiting to join a convoy. He described a convoy of which he had recently been part where after just three days out one ship had struck a mine and sunk, the tanker just ahead had been torpedoed and his ship had also been torpedoed, flinging him across the bridge resulting in a night on a raft when he was too cold to open its food supply.

On 18 September the *Aldershot News* celebrated what they considered to be a long overdue increase in soldiers' pay. Serving soldiers with families were under pressure to adequately provide for them on existing levels of pay. Understandably this raises the question of whether the government's oft-stated concern about the welfare of its soldiers was somewhat superficial. Clearly those working in the industries associated with the war effort were far better remunerated. For instance, new recruits were being paid up to £8 a week for activities such as tea-making. Unfortunately for the coalition government, its proposal on soldiers' pay was torn to shreds in Parliament because its approach of dressing up the pay levels to seem larger than they really were was questioned. The grudging way in which serving soldiers were paid reflected back to the way army pay had been depressed right up to the outbreak of war in 1939.

In reviewing 1942, the local paper in its customary review of the preceding year, made mention of the men and women from its circulation area that had served in places such as the Middle East and would never return. Mention was also made of the raising of £175,000 for the submarine *Tuna*. The Tanks for Victory appeal had raised £83,000 which resulted in three of the army's tanks carrying Aldershot's name. Fund-raising through a penny a week campaign was aimed at producing parcels for PoWs in Germany and Italy. Support for the Soviet Union in July was reflected in the raising of £1,500 for an X-ray machine in November. This had been preceded by an Anglo-Soviet week in May in which the Minister for Production, the Rt Hon. Oliver Lyttelton PC, Aldershot's Member of Parliament, linked the challenge of the forthcoming eighty days with the struggle going on in the Soviet Union against the might of the Germans. 'Today the Germans are thrusting towards Stalingrad in their attempt to sever communications of the Russian army from the oilfields in the Caucasus,' he told a large audience in Manor Park. 'So these are very tense days and one watches with admiration the stubborn resistance which the Russian armies are putting up on an enormous front.' The council supplied a lorry with a huge skull-and-crossbones encouraging people to recycle their paper as well as rags, bones and tins. Speaking again in Aldershot in June to the Aldershot Conservative Association, Mr Lyttelton highlighted the productive capacity of Britain which had exceeded the three Axis powers of Germany, Italy and Japan. He praised American mass-production with their Liberty ships (low-cost cargo vessels) and in aircraft production: one bomber every hour. There were 22 million people in Britain between the ages of 14 and 65 in full-time employment out of a cohort of 33 million. He went on to detail the self-denial being made for the war effort with those on higher incomes paying tax of 19/6d in the pound and the whole population subject to strict rationing.

At the end of 1942 news of the success of the Hampshire Regiment in Tunisia was received. The Hampshire Regiment had landed in Algeria to form the spearhead for attacks on the Axis in Bizerte and Tunis. By 29 November the Hampshires were in close contact with the enemy. The *Aldershot News* accused the military authorities of suppressing the news of the Hampshires. *The Times* reported their achievement from November 29 when they took up a position in a wood by the Jedeida-Tebourba road. It was the most advanced position and was overlooked by the enemy. Throughout the next day the Hampshires were plastered with machine-gun and mortar fire. On the western side a young officer had only five men to defend his position and had to make a bayonet charge to drive the Germans back. In this engagement he and his five men knocked out two enemy tanks with anti-tank rifles and mortars. During the following three days the battalion was subject to attack from tanks and mortar fire supported by infantry. On the second day the German tanks attacking from the left bank overran their trenches but were driven back with the loss of six tanks. This degree of heroism could not save them from an impossible position. A bayonet charge on the left flank wiped out three German machine-gun posts, but they had to give way. The newspaper demanded to know why the name of the regiment who fought a desperate hand-to-hand battle for four days and nights and who broke up direct infantry attacks with bayonet charges was suppressed. As the Germans had blocked the road out of the area they were defending, the Hampshires' colonel told his men they could surrender or break into twos and threes in order to escape, ignoring German invitations to surrender.

A test was conducted on Aldershot's ARP system and although it was not numerically strong it came up to the required standard. Reflecting the increasing role women were playing in wartime Hampshire, Aldershot's fire-watching provision had been strengthened by the registration of 5,000 women between the ages of 20 and 45. Claims were made of real progress in nursery provision during the year to support mothers increasingly involved in important war work. A girls' training course had been established during the year, together with a cadet unit in Aldershot to support the Hampshire Regiment.

Entering 1943 there were signs that after the threat of invasion normal political comment was resuming. Sergeant G. Waller wrote to the *Aldershot News* complaining that the government had shelved the recommendations of the Beveridge Report in a letter that pointed to the difference between the lives of soldiers and civilian workers. On 19 March, thirteen months before it happened, discussion about the invasion of France began to be highlighted at a meeting at Farnborough Town Hall, possibly reflecting the pressure Stalin was placing on the Allies to open a second front. Military success had meant that most of the coastline of North Africa was in Allied hands and the next step appeared to be the invasion of Sicily. However, more mundane issues relating to the challenge of feeding people in the Aldershot area were of greater consequence. The education committee was debating the amount that parents with children in receipt of school meals in the town's elementary schools should be asked to pay. Previously the charge had been based around the cost of the food and part of the overhead charges of the preparation and cooking. A new law stated that only the cost of the food should be paid for and not any other overheads involved. On 30 April the *Aldershot News* criticized this on the basis that wealthier families would be only too pleased to pay the full cost and that the new law wasted public money. It also defended the school dinners being served against charges that they were of a poor standard by saying that they were of a good standard. Corporate concerns also centred on the shortage of manpower. There was an acute shortage of men available for essential maintenance work in the borough. Aldershot had been allowed ninety-one men for essential maintenance. In response to their letter to the Ministry of Labour the council achieved the promise of the loan of men over 50 years of age.

The third birthday of the Home Guard was marked in Aldershot, Farnborough and Fleet. Recruiting men from age 17 to 60 at the beginning of the year, local groups now armed with modern weapons were on parade displaying their efficiency and competence. In Aldershot the Home Guard marched from their headquarters in Elm Place to the recreation ground where they provided an exhibition featuring the way in which they had acquired military skills. Moving on to Manor Park they gave an exhibition of how an effective defence against enemy tanks could be conducted. Realism was created by the use of smoke bombs. At Farnborough, A and B companies were on parade and marched to Osborne Road recreation ground to provide an example of weapons training and battle drill. At Fleet, C Company assembled at the cricket ground where they carried out a realistic training exercise involving an attack on a group of paratroopers who had landed near a farmhouse at the end of the ground.

Some of the voices of 1943 Hampshire came from men who were PoWs in Germany, Italy and the Far East. The *Aldershot News* carried a photo of the men in Stalag 383. J. Penfold was a professional soldier who had served in India, Palestine and Aldershot. He had been taken prisoner during the evacuation of Crete. In the camp he had formed a band. His wife was resident in Basingstoke and they had a boy he had never seen. Corporal W. Croucher served as a drummer in the 2nd Dorsetshire Regimental Band. He was captured at Dunkirk. In Italy Trooper Oliver Callingham from Farnborough sent a picture of himself and other PoWs from Camp PG 70.PM 3300 based near the Adriatic Coast. He was captured in the Middle East in June 1942. Next to him was Jack Tisley who again was captured in the Middle East in September 1942 and whose wife and daughter lived in Frimley Green. Corporal Tisley's brother was aged 20 when he was killed at Dunkirk. There is little evidence of photos from the Far East, possibly because the treatment received by PoWs was so grim that the camera could not disguise the awful reality of their treatment.

Summarizing Aldershot's contribution to the war effort in 1943, the *Aldershot News* highlighted its war savings which it claimed were equal to the best in the country. A total of £2.5 million had been raised in that year alone. A total of 72 employment groups had been involved with 2,736 members and 20 school groups with 2,365 members contributing. However, most contributions came from savers outside any savings organization. Since the beginning of the war to December 1942, £2.7 million had been raised. Physical contribution towards armaments had come through four Lancaster bombers and a £25,000 contribution towards troop-carrying gliders. On the down side, difficulties were experienced with the school meals service when the education committee was told by government that the cost to families must be mainly for the cost of the food and not overheads. To date Aldershot had only experienced 9 raids and 28 bombs, resulting in 4 killed and 77 injured. Already plans were being worked on for 'welcome home' ceremonies for the men and women from the borough. Plans were afoot to give Churchill the freedom of the borough. Aldershot Hospital had been called upon to treat those injured by flying bombs. An essential contribution towards the war effort was what could be done locally towards food production. The local Horticultural Society, the Allotments Association, the Poultry and Rabbit

Club and the Beekeepers' Association all promoted the local production of food. For the 300 allotments, supplies of lime and fertilizers were made available together with the raising and selling of plants. The Poultry and Rabbit Club ensured an improvement in the quality of laying hens, as well as producing a supply of rabbit meat locally.

Allotments came to play an important role in the survival of families as rationing continued to limit the food supply. In the Farnborough and Cove area cultivating an allotment became part of the way of life assisted by bulk-buying of seeds and practical advice given by the Farnborough and Cove Allotments Society. Any arable areas such as football pitches went under the spade. Despite wartime difficulties the August agricultural show for Farnborough and Cove continued with prizes for fruit, vegetables and flowers. As well as this, home-made products such as jam and honey were on display.

It should be remembered that for every kilogram of food consumed, a seaman put his life on the line because of the country's dependence on the food supply from abroad. A way of life in Hampshire became the coupon book from which dockets for food were torn. Top of the list for rationing were butter, sugar, bacon and ham, but by 1940 meat, tea, margarine and lard had been added. By 1941 eggs, jam and milk had joined them in the ration books. In Hampshire a typical weekly ration amounted to 2oz of tea, 8oz of sugar, 4oz of jam and 2oz of lard, margarine and butter. If households were fortunate enough to find them, 4oz of cheese and bacon, one egg and 1lb of meat could be had. A meat sandwich was half the meat ration. Apart from those supplied to troops serving abroad, cigarettes were only available 'under the counter'. Also it is little wonder that American troops were so popular with children because when sweets were rationed they became the supply of 'candy' for children in Hampshire. The usual dessert in Hampshire households was based on apples which in many parts of the county were readily available in the garden. Where there was no apple harvest, families benefited from other families with more apples than they needed. Even in suburban Cove, residents could witness piglets being driven from Parsonage pig farm with youngsters running ahead of the procession to ensure they did not escape. The pigs were fed with pig swill collected from army barracks at Pinehurst, Deepcut and Blackdown that was boiled up in cauldrons with cereal and meal added to them. From the Tank Corps Barracks' cookhouse came a regular supply of swill rewarded by Mr Harvey with a donation towards the cookhouse fund.

Canteen service workers with the WRVS.

Members of the Land Army.

A well-earned cuppa for the troops provided by the WRVS.

A canteen where workers listened to Workers' Playtime *on the radio.*

CHAPTER SEVENTEEN

Hampshire Hero:
Syd Hewson, RN

Syd Hewson was born in Nottinghamshire and at 14 he left school to join the hosiery trade working in the quality control department. When he was 17, encouraged by an uncle, he applied to join the Royal Navy. He was turned down because he was partly colour-blind. However, the following year, knowing he would shortly be conscripted he applied again and was immediately accepted.

Syd was sent for training to HMS *Collingwood* in Portsmouth. Among his intake he was by far the youngest. Ahead of him were twelve weeks of intensive training. This coincided with some of the worst blitz activity in the Portsmouth area. Collingwood was attacked and some of its buildings destroyed. There was a rota requiring that two of the trainees remain outside the air-raid shelter in case of fire. If bombing was taking place in Portsmouth they did not go into town to the pubs and dances. Collingwood's NAAFI could provide beer for the recruits anyway. Part of their training involved rowing a whaleboat on the front at Southsea. On one occasion when Syd was doing this, the petty officer in charge pointed to a tanker refuelling in the harbour. Suddenly there was a flash and it blew up. A large part of the harbour was on fire from burning oil. They started to row towards what remained of the tanker but were overtaken by motor boats that had rushed forward. The tanker had struck a magnetic mine laid in the harbour the previous night by the Germans.

Just eight weeks into his course Syd was picked out to travel to Douglas on the Isle of Man to be trained as a radar technician. This was to take place at HMS *Valkyrie* which turned out to be a castle on the hill and the secret Radar Training Quarters up to which they were marched each morning at 6.30

Syd Hewson, Légion d'Honneur.

am from hotels along the front in Douglas. Training involved cruising up and down the west coast outside Liverpool being instructed in early radar technology. After training it was back to Portsmouth to await posting to ships on which they would serve. They were desperately needed, as a close friend was immediately flown out to Malta. One morning an officer appeared with a clipboard instructing them that they should report forthwith to Glasgow from where they would be allocated their ships. Although Syd was the youngest, he was picked out to shepherd his party to Glasgow.

Syd's ship turned out to be HMS *Glasgow*. This was a ship he described as 'only holding together by the paint that had recently been applied to it.' Built in 1915, she had been salvaged from the Delaware River where she had languished since 1918 because the value of her steel did not merit her being broken up. So the vessel had been mothballed. She was one of the forty-odd ships given to Britain as part of the Lend-Lease scheme. Summoned on board he was presented with a set of keys to the radar locker and told to 'get on with it'. A problem immediately arose in that he was still an ordinary seaman responsible for a demanding role. This was solved by defining him as the navigating officer's yeoman. One of the responsibilities of the job involved drawing up charts locating where the many ships sunk during this period had gone down.

The radar worked through a winding device. At the lower level it was designed to identify surface shipping. The signal received was a straight line on a small screen with another ship disturbing the line. At the top of the ship's mast was the part of the device designed to detect aircraft. This operated over just 10,000 yards. This would give the commander about one and a half minute's warning of an approaching plane. When indication appeared on Syd's screen, only then did he communicate with the bridge through an open tube. However, this could not be kept open because it would fill with water in rough weather. The ship also had electronic equipment for detecting submarines and carried depth-charges. His duties were four hours on and four hours off when the ship was at sea, winding the aerial to the equipment by hand.

Syd was assigned to a new ship HMS *Brighton* working with the North Atlantic convoys. The ship helped in the evacuation of the occupying force from Iceland when the Americans took over. In the process of doing this she was rammed and very badly holed in the stern by another ship. *Brighton* immediately began to take on water and the crew's task was to get her back to port. For the next few days the crew lived with water up to their knees, having to hang up their sea boots before climbing into their hammocks. Fresh water was only available for one hour in the morning and one hour at night because the water tanks had to supplement the ship's fuel tanks because they only allowed for a limited amount of travel and the crew had to exist on cold food. A Sunderland flying boat occasionally checked if they were still afloat as they limped back to Britain. In recognition of this, the navy dusted down an allowance not used since Nelson's time to pay the crew one shilling per day.

On reaching port Syd was signed off and had three weeks' home leave.

Syd's next ship was HMS *Cockatrice*, a purpose-built mine-sweeper. She swept for mines in the Channel and for D-Day the ship arrived at Ryde ready to sweep ahead of the invasion fleet from there to GOLD Beach. Off the Normandy coast *Cockatrice* swept the sea for the next two weeks. This was part of what was known as the Piccadilly Circus of ships accumulated along the French coast supplying support for the 100,000 men who landed there. On one occasion the destroyer next to *Cockatrice* suddenly blew up, probably after being torpedoed. Amid the indescribable noise *Cockatrice* assisted in the rescue of the stricken ship. There was then continual work sweeping the Channel in order to ensure the smooth supply of Allied troops in France.

Towards the end of the war *Cockatrice* was involved in occupying the German port of Cuxhaven in advance of the British army landing there. There was no German resistance, except that out of the blue a German dispatch rider appeared. After he ignored an order to surrender he was shot, but his state-of-the-art motorbike was taken and raffled among the ship's petty officers. *Cockatrice* then returned to Harwich and two days later Germany surrendered and the war in Europe ended.

On VE Day Syd was in Chatham and assigned to barracks there. He was about to begin training to become a petty officer and then be sent to the Pacific to prepare for the invasion of Japan. However, Japan's surrender meant that this was cancelled and he was stuck in a chaotic Chatham asked to accommodate hundreds of servicemen pouring back from all over the world. Fortunately Syd met one of the officers with whom he had served on HMS *Brighton* who was about to be demobbed from his role in the Chatham barracks of signing off supplies coming off ships being mothballed. During this period, as far as the navy was concerned he had disappeared. He arranged for his post to be passed on to Syd and here he happily existed until his name appeared among those being demobbed.

As for HMS *Brighton*, she was transferred to the Russians in July 1944 and on her return to the Royal Navy after the war she was broken up. *Cockatrice* survived until the 1950s when she too was broken up.

Syd has just received the Légion d'Honneur order of merit from the government of France.

CHAPTER EIGHTEEN

Hampshire's Canoeist Raiders

The concept of this commando raid on the crucially important naval port of Bordeaux in south-west France came from Hampshire and the Portsmouth suburb of Southsea to be exact. The men who formed the raiding party became known as the Cockleshell Heroes, much to the annoyance of the developer of the raid Herbert 'Blondie' Hasler. Its code-name was Operation FRANKTON. The justification for it arose through a number of Axis attacks using mini-submarines and small ships in the Mediterranean in particular. At the low ebb of the war the search was on for activity which could be seen as taking the fight to the enemy. A larger attack with even graver consequences was the raid on Dieppe.

The idea was the brainchild of the distinguished Royal Marines officer Lieutenant Colonel Hasler who had been awarded the OBE for bravery in the Norway campaign and it grew out of his passion for canoeing and small boats. The objective was for the raiders to attach limpet mines to the docked German cargo ships and then escape overland to Spain. Hasler's first task was to locate suitable canoes that would take a team of twelve men in six two-man canoes up the Gironde Estuary for four days, heading for Bordeaux harbour. The canoes would have to be stored effectively on HMS *Tuna*, the submarine designated to be the launch-pad off the Gironde Estuary. Several types of canoes were considered including the German Klipper, a Canadian canoe and one used by Scott in the Antarctic but in the end one specially designed by Hasler was built by Sevo Laminated Workshop Limited, a local firm. It needed to have a flat bottom to enable it to be pulled over shingle. On 26 January 1942, Hasler set about recruiting a team for the raid. The men would be formed around Commando Unit 101 and were based in an office in Nissen huts just opposite the boating lake. Hasler spent much of the time prior to the raid deliberately seeking to penetrate the harbour patrols around the Solent and Hayling Island. He advertised for volunteers within the Royal Marine Patrol Detachment who were indifferent to personal safety and were free of strong family ties. He was not overwhelmed with men coming forward but he believed he had a good cross-section of 'average young fellows'. The Boom Patrol detachment was formed on 6 July 1942. What was quickly apparent was the lack of boating experience among Hasler's men and some of his men, billeted in a guest house on the Worthing Road, could not even swim. However, the emphasis was on the men's overall physical fitness and their ability to operate in a situation demanding stealth.

Lieutenant Colonel Herbert 'Blondie' Hasler, commander of Operation FRANKTON.

The proposal to proceed with the raid was turned down by the majority of the Admiralty Committee examining it but was saved when it received Lord Mountbatten's support. Unfortunately the absolute failure of a trial operated between Margate and Deptford canoeing up the Swale was disregarded and the raid went ahead with six canoes with two men in each. The men were kitted out with sea boots, stockings, battle-class trousers, gym shoes, waders, woollen vests, roll-neck sweaters, life-jackets and two pairs of gloves. They were armed with a .45 pistol, a knife and a bird-call whistle. However, there were problems almost from the commencement of the raid when the canoeists left the submarine on 7 December 1942 and paddled towards the estuary. One of the canoes was ripped as it was taken out of the submarine and had to be withdrawn with its two-man crew. They had also been spotted by a German aircraft. Now down to five canoes and ten men, they lost contact with each other as they attempted to surf the huge swells over 5ft high at the mouth of the estuary. One of the canoes foundered and the bodies of its crew were washed up along the coast. Another capsized and its crew had to cling to the surviving canoes until they could swim to the coast but later died of hypothermia. The remaining crews slipped past the two frigates at the mouth of the estuary by the men lying flat and paddling silently. After paddling for four nights two of the canoes reached Bordeaux where they managed to attach limpet mines to a number of ships. Those who were caught by the Germans were summarily executed under the instruction of the commander of the German navy, Admiral Erich Raeder. Because of British incompetence, the fact that the French Resistance were about to attack Bordeaux at the same time was never revealed to the Marines. Only Hasler and Bill Sparks, his No. 2, returned from the raid.

Two members of the Operation FRANKTON Commando group.

Lieutenant Colonel Hasler, who was one of only two survivors of Operation FRANKTON.

CHAPTER NINETEEN

Hampshire Women's Crucial Role

In 1939 there was a paucity of opportunity open to Hampshire's women in terms of work. For many it was simply a case of going into domestic service, which meant giving up not only their working lives but also their private lives to middle- and upper-class families. There had been some changes as a result of the demands for labour during the Great War but the 1920s and part of the 1930s had seen a retreat from this progress. For married women the expectation was of their place being in the home but the fierce crucible of war and the problem of maintaining a viable society when a large part of the population was in the armed forces brought about dramatic change. An important factor in this was the role played in the coalition government by Labour figures such as Ernest Bevin who came from a Party commitment to the advancement of women in society. Shortly after the start of the war, women quickly slipped once again into occupations in which they had replaced men during the Great War, such as conductors on buses and trains. Their becoming drivers was slightly delayed but was taking place in Portsmouth by 1940. What was more important was the systematic recruitment of women and their mobilization into the workforce where questions had to be asked about why they were not employed in male-dominated roles such as flying planes.

Not only was the female working life changing but their domestic role now expanded into operating mobile canteens and providing back-up services during the cruellest air-raids in Portsmouth, Southampton and Gosport. The important support services for the army, navy and Air Force were taken over by the Women's Royal Naval Service (WRNS, popularly known as Wrens), WAAFS and the ATS and the women working with the anti-aircraft guns in Hampshire. For many of these women, these activities had to take place in conjunction with overcoming the restrictions and complications of living in wartime Britain. By 1944, out of the 22 million in employment or in the forces in Britain, 7 million were women. Bevin commented: 'Cheerfully and willingly they have taken their part in the war effort at great inconvenience.' Those working at factories such as Wellworthys in Lymington faced long hours, sometimes up to seventy hours per week. On top of this they had to endure the pain and distress relating to loved ones and men from their community who were injured or had died. Joyce Carlisle, aged 99 at the time of writing, still speaks of how many young men from her class at Brockenhurst Grammar School went down with HMS *Hood* when the ship was sunk in 1940.

Pioneering women pilots at a Hampshire airfield.

When women were witnessed producing essential parts for Spitfires at Woolston, no longer could they be dismissed as the little women in the advertisements appearing in Hampshire's newspapers. Despite this propaganda, government sources were still suggesting that because women were responsible for curtains in their household, they should take responsibility for that household's blackout. For the women cleaning and maintaining steam locomotives in Eastleigh's railway workshops, attitudes such as this were treated with rightful derision. Like Rosy the Riveter in America, many of these women went on to become skilled fitters and mechanics putting in a twelve-hour day. A reporter visiting the workshop commented on how the young workers there still managed to be immaculately turned out, despite the grease and dirt with which they worked. Other jobs on Hampshire's railways such as porters, enquiry and ticket office workers, staff at freight depots and warehouses were also taken over by women. They began to be trained to operate the signals as well as driving delivery vans throughout Hampshire. Portsmouth was distinguished by being the first place to appoint a woman to drive a double-decker bus. Two women drivers, Mrs E.V. Hunt and Mrs

K.E. Devine, in 1941 drove double-deckers through Portsmouth during the worst of the blitz. Anyone fortunate enough to obtain fuel for their car at this time might have come across women painting white lines on the Hampshire/ Sussex border or young members of the Women's Timber Corps (WTC) in Hampshire cutting timber to be used in Mosquito aircraft. In order to prevent wastage of nuts and bolts dropped during manufacturing, women at Wickham organized a group to pick up fallen nuts, bolts and screws from factory floors, meaning that skilled workers no longer had to be taken off production lines to retrieve such materials.

It had quickly become apparent, due to the country's dependence on supplies from overseas, that food would have to be rationed. It was vital that through allotments, bringing neglected land back into use and replacing agricultural labourers who had been called up, the Land Army in Hampshire would have to raise as much locally-produced food as possible. By 1941 the Women's Land Army had 12,000 members with a joining rate of 500 per month. As with engineering, these volunteers acquired a whole range of rural skills such as ditching, hedging and milking. The Land Army also had to deal with the integration of black volunteers when their administrators refused to accept such people from East London. A farmer in Wickham agreed to accept one on his farm and four villagers offered her accommodation. Pam from Cove described a 'rude awakening' when having signed up to become a Land Girl, a ticket to Ipswich in Suffolk arrived. Out of the £2.00 she received, she was expected to pay 25 shillings for board and keep. The discipline they experienced was not as strict as in the services or working in a factory and they usually had Saturday and Sunday off. She would have liked to travel home but could not afford it. As the war went on, the need for women with childcare responsibilities to join the workforce became urgent, as did the need for nurseries. Aldershot and Portsmouth councils began to take responsibility for providing nurseries from 1943 onwards.

It was the WVS that provided the backbone for communities under the stress of total war, whether it was through knitting socks and clothing for the navy and airmen or supplying hospitals with a steady stream of sterile dressings. The abiding image of the WVS is of women standing ready with the teapot at the numerous canteens they provided throughout Hampshire. They also provided much of the leadership in moves to collect material such as aluminium used in aircraft manufacture and rope for camouflage nets around anti-aircraft guns. Women offering a whole range of technical skills were recruited for Southwick where the whole D-Day operation was being coordinated.

Britain leapt into the lead by beginning to employ women to fly military aircraft from the factories where they were being produced to their operational airfield. The movement towards this started before the war when Sir Gerard d'Erlanger recognized that there was likely to be an important role for amateur pilots in the event of war. He wrote to the Air Ministry suggesting a role for non-military pilots in moving aircraft to places where they would become operational as well as delivering supplies to the country's airfields. D'Erlanger had become Director of British Airways Limited and was charged with putting his idea into practice. In September 1939, when it became apparent that more of these pilots were required, the decision was made to extend recruitment to female pilots. Women came forward from a distinguished heritage which included Amy Johnson and New Zealander Jean Batten. Pauline Gower was given the task of recruiting eight women pilots who became familiar sights at Hampshire's airfields, among other things delivering new planes from Supermarine. Women workers played an essential role at the victualling base, the Royal Clarence Yard. This involved preparing the rum ration for distribution. Betty Marshall from Havant was employed in making gliders for Operation OVERLORD and remembers that at Airspeed their factory was under great pressure to complete Horsa gliders. The woods around Rowland's Castle, Havant and Finchdean were packed with troops, guns and tanks. On 5 June she was able to observe hundreds of gliders being towed towards France. Despite this, she only became aware that D-Day was happening when Churchill's speech was relayed on the tannoy at Airspeed.

'I only joined for the hat....' Hazel Russell went to Fort Blockhouse in Gosport for two weeks' training after joining the WRNS in 1943. She was 21 and had been working as a secretary in London as well as working as a driver for the YMCA driving to AA sites with refreshments. She was one of six Wrens who replaced sailors on a simulator for submarine training and who, by November 1941, were working at Dolphin Quay on the simulator located over two floors. This consisted of a rotating conning tower, a periscope and a fruit machine-type analogue computer that provided target conditions. On the upper floor targets moved along railway tracks. She and her fellow Wrens slept at the simulator. Security for the whole operation was very tight because it incorporated all the latest thinking in submarine technology.

Throughout Hampshire women came forward as nurses. One of Hampshire's VADs describes joining the Red Cross in 1936, aware that war was likely. Passing the VAD exams required spending considerable amounts of time working in a Lymington hospital. This involved cycling 14 miles each month to work on the wards as a probationer. When war was declared she joined the RAMC at the Military Hospital at Netley. She was with seventy other VADs from all walks of life and some even dating from the Great War. After six weeks they were put on night duty which was from 8.00 pm to 8.00 am with just a thirty-minute break. There was an appalling lack of equipment and they were quartered in old barracks with two outside toilets and only cold water from taps with tin basins. Only two baths were available, neither with a plug. Faced with this experience, the urge came to return to farming and she resigned from the Red Cross and joined the Land Army.

Joan David spoke of arriving at Aldershot to join the ATS and seeing the wretched condition of the men evacuated from Dunkirk, half-naked and utterly exhausted. She hurriedly organized an appeal for clothes for them. Thelma Ryder, originally from Plymouth, joined Wellworthys in Lymington making piston rings. Her mother cried when she saw her in her factory overalls, believing that she had cast aside all femininity. Thelma remembered Wellworthys as a friendly society with pay on a piecework basis. However, no protective masks were provided, despite the real danger of a splinter of steel lodging in workers' eyes. Maureen Bolster treasured Christmas 1945 when she stumbled around distributing presents and started the day with a real egg for breakfast. Wendy Maddox, who was born in Aldershot, remembers being in a shelter behind her house in Basingstoke until there was a shelter inside their house. She recalled a plane falling from the sky with a parachutist falling with it. One day, just after being called inside because it was getting dark, a plane went machine-gunning along their street. Marjorie Toomer joined the Land Army in Ealing and after studying at Oakfield College near St Albans in dairying, pig and poultry training she began to work on Hampshire farms. Before the war she had lived in Andover and was pleased to return there with the Land Army. Unfortunately she developed a disease associated with cows and was moved to horticultural work, mainly sprout-picking, near Staines.

Mrs E. Hooper recalled joining the Land Army and remembers picking potatoes and having to sort out the good ones from the rotten ones. She went on to working with cows, spending an hour milking and then going out to the fields to hoe. 'If you cleaned out the manure you were likely to end up with a face full of muck and you had to learn to use a pitchfork for haymaking in a proper way.' Mrs Ros Smisson had tried to join the WRNS but was turned down and sent to the Land Army as a rat-catcher. The pest control unit operated out of Winchester, sending people out to farms in gangs of four. Their vans contained two dilapidated bins, one of bait and the other of cyanide.

Naina A. Cox was aged 16 at the time of D-Day and worked in the accounts section of a dry cleaners in Portsmouth. She had been actively engaged with the local Red Cross and had recently qualified in her first-aid exams. At 2.00 pm on 6 June Miss Hobbs, who was one of the tutors of her group, had urgently sought her out to be at Queen Alexander hospital by 5.00 pm. By 6.00 pm she was busy dressing the first gunshot wound she had ever dealt with and realized who was in the constant stream of convoys of lorries passing by her family home. Such was the volume of wounded that stretchers had to be left in corridors. Her job was to clean up patients, most of whom were grimy and covered in blood. Naina worked for days without a break and she began to feel that her work would never stop. She was working with traumatized men covered in excrement. Then she was asked to work with German prisoners located in a foul-smelling Nissen hut. 'One of the rules of the Red Cross is that you are there to help everyone. I'm glad I didn't refuse to help those young men.' She remembered the long silences in that ward and the pathetic grey young faces.

Much of the comment about social life in the Second World War spotlights the dances and the new sense of freedom now available to women, many of whom had been lifted out of their domestic circumstances. In Hampshire the resulting liaisons produced scores of children as well as GI brides ostentatiously leaving for the supposed bright lights of America from Southampton. On the darker side, there were the women seeking to terminate their unplanned pregnancies at a time when abortion was still a criminal offence. Joyce Carlisle from Burley talks about the trauma of V, a woman who had an affair with a married Irish labourer working on airport construction. She was billeted in the spare room when she attempted to abort the baby she was carrying and nearly lost her life. In the case of D, whose mother fell pregnant as a result of her relationship with a Canadian soldier, the relationship changed her mother's life for the worse. This was no affair between a soldier and a local girl both in their twenties. D's mother was 35 and her lover the same age. He was married and had five children back in Toronto. D's mother had met J in Basingstoke when she was helping out in a paint and decorating shop. D thinks her father was probably a wireless operator based in Aldershot but what she has been able to find out about J is scarce and often contradictory. Her mother either refused or was unable to give D complete details of her father and D had to embark on a long quest between 1986 and 1990 to find any information. She did discover that J's mother in Canada had sent her mother food parcels when she had made contact with her, complaining as a single mother in 1945 that she was destitute and living in a local environment censorious of women having children out of wedlock. There is some indication of J suffering from shellshock as a result of the Anzio landings in Italy and being hospitalized because of this. Despite the heartbreak involved, for the rest of her life D's mother always spoke of J as being the only love of her life, although she married someone else after the war. There was some compensation for D in being able to travel to Canada to meet her half-brothers and sisters. Historian Arthur Marwick makes the point that post-war paternalism soon swept away many of the apparent advances made by women during the Second World War.

Nurses at Aldershot Hospital.

Members of the Hampshire Land Army.

Land Army worker.

Women volunteers (WRVS) loading supplies.

CHAPTER TWENTY

The Island That Got in the Way

A grievous error made by military planners prior to the Second World War was to assume that the Isle of Wight would not be a strategic target for aerial attack. Perhaps they should have consulted a map and observed its position in direct line for any attack on the major targets of Portsmouth and Southampton. While the damage inflicted on the island was not nearly as great as that on Portsmouth and Southampton, from the outbreak of war to the turn of the tide for the war in 1942, the people of the island suffered considerably from the attention of the Luftwaffe. It was natural that because of its location, rightly or wrongly it was seen to some extent as a shield for mainland Britain. In September 1938 when the Munich Agreement was being debated in the House of Commons, a member of Chamberlain's Cabinet referring to the part of Czechoslovakia occupied by a largely German population compared that area to the Isle of Wight.

Air-raid precautions had been in place for some time but on 11 March 1938 an island-wide exercise marking the appointment of a full-time ARP officer took place. Even then, it still did not include a compulsory blackout requirement, only a request that householders should spill as little light as possible. However, planners were faced with a government contention stating that the island was not a vulnerable area and therefore no resources were to be made available for air-raid shelters. The counter-argument pointing to the island's direct flight path to Portsmouth and Southampton fell on deaf ears. In September 1938 a full exercise was organized involving gas contamination squads, full-time firemen and auxiliary firemen, the police and special constabulary, first-aid and ambulance services and the hospital at Ryde.

Yet the likely advent of war still did not deter hundreds of holidaymakers from swarming all over the island among the men beginning to man the gun emplacements and searchlight units. Only when war was declared was the Isle of Wight authorized to build shelters at its schools and for the 10 per cent of people it was believed would be caught on the streets during an attack. Despite the fact that the island was just thirty minutes away from the mainland, it was chosen as a place to evacuate children. Contrary to the official view, important ship-building and aircraft manufacture took place at Cowes and at St Boniface Down an important part of the radar chain was located. An indication that parents in Gosport and Southampton felt that evacuation to somewhere so close was misguided was indicated as although a packed first boat arrived on day one, subsequent boats on that day were barely half full, with just 4,040 out of 8,600 arriving on the island. The percentage of evacuees arriving on day two was even lower with only 1,070 out of 5,700 arriving. The control room for managing civil defence was in Newport and from there the supplies for this radiated. Appeals for auxiliary firemen and wardens were well supported. The first air-raid warning came in at 6.42 am on 6 September 1939 and although it was a false alarm there was an effective response; a warning of the release of mustard gas proved probably to be garlic. Indeed, the council had to dispel the rumour that meteorological balloons found on some of the beaches contained poison gas. In the grip of bitter winter weather on 6 January 1940 an Avro Anson aircraft from Thorney Island's 48 Squadron crashed into St Catherine's Down, killing its pilot and all but one of its crew members, signalling the commencement of aircraft incidents that would last throughout the war.

The first shooting down of an aircraft was mistakenly reported as being German but it turned out to be a British aircraft. It was a Fairey light bomber from the 12th Operational Training Unit based at Andover and although its pilot survived, its crew members were both killed. On 14 June 1940 the first high-explosive bombs fell on the island, coming from a single raider on a probing mission. As the Germans swept through France, the island took on the character of a fortress despite frequent bombing and at first there was little damage being done. However, all this was to change from 2 July 1940 when for two years the island became Hell's Corner. There is evidence that the island was marked as a strategic target on German maps in Admiral Raeder's first plans for the invasion of Britain, although these were later amended. There were, however, plans for a landing at Selsey which was close to the island. Because of its strategic position it could not be immune to the naval events taking place around its coastline and in the air above it as well as aircraft activity onshore. For instance, on 27 July a Vickers Vildebeest Allied plane crashed in sight of Yarmouth Pier. On 8 August 1940 a German plane crash-landed on the island intact with its bombs still on board. It had been forced to crash-land by a Hurricane P3896 from 145 Squadron flying out of Westhampnett. This was the only plane shot down that day to land on the island. On 11 August radar picked up 170 bombers with fighter escort approaching the island and 70 Hurricanes and Spitfires were soon airborne to intercept them. One plane crash-landed and burst into flames, killing its pilot when one of its wings caught fire.

Although the Germans were unsure about how the British radar system operated, they realized that the radar station and masts at Boniface Down, St Catherine's Bay were a vital part of its operation. On 12 August 1940 it was heavily bombed, most of the service buildings around the station being destroyed. There was extensive use of delayed-action bombs. Despite this the radar station was still able to operate, prompting an enemy return on 16

August to finish off the site and black out the radar. On the same day a mine-sweeper was machine-gunned off East Cowes and later sunk and casualties were brought ashore. The island seemed to provide a curtain-raiser for attacks around Portsmouth and the Solent with raids on Thorney Island, Lee-on-Solent and Gosport on 18 August which meant that Newport was machine-gunned almost as an afterthought. By the time the focus of the German attacks had switched to London on 15 August, there had been 245 air-raid warnings on the island. On 28 November a German air ace, *Kommodore* Helmut Wick who was aged just 22, was flying at the head of a force of Bf 109s. He claimed fifty-six Allied aircraft shot down. There is still a debate regarding which plane from 609 Squadron shot him down, his plane plunging into the sea just off St Catherine's Point. None of the pilots involved in the fierce aerial fighting of that day lived to recall the exact details of what happened.

All this was to be shaded into relative insignificance by distraught watchers from the island who witnessed what was happening to Portsmouth on Wednesday, 10 January 1940. Ernie Jolliffe told of his frustration at not being able to go across the Solent and offer assistance: 'We watched Portsmouth burn. The sky turned completely red. We wanted to do something, to go over there and help, but were told it would do no good because we didn't know the lie of the land and would only get in the way of the rescue operation.' There was no safety even for the children who had been evacuated from Portsmouth for on 4 April John Farrari, a 16-year-old evacuee, was killed at Yafford. There was always an inherent risk involved in manning searchlights illustrated on 15 March 1941 when a direct hit killed three soldiers. The island was suffering because aircraft returning from raids would jettison their bombs before crossing over to France. With the formation of the Home Guard there was a belief that they would be tenacious in the defence of the place where they grew up. Perhaps their greatest contribution was involvement in the defence of the radar unit at St Boniface, near Ventnor, part of the national radar chain consisting of eight pylons, thirty-five steel masts and wooden huts housing the technical staff.

As previously mentioned, intensive maritime activity was constantly taking place around the island. At 4.00 am on 20 September 1940, the Southern paddle-steamer *Portsdown* left Portsmouth Harbour as part of its ferry link with Ryde. A scraping noise was heard on its port side followed by an explosion. It had hit a mine off Spitbank Fort, Southsea. Seventeen people were saved but up to fourteen passengers and eight of the ship's crew perished. On the night of 10/11 November six British airmen from the thirty-seven bomber crews reported missing after heavy raids on Berlin and other parts of Germany late that night drifted ashore at Steel Bay near Ventnor. They had paddled their rubber dinghy 150 to 200 miles following the crash of their Wellington bomber 30 miles from the Thames Estuary. The airmen had been too weak even to pull the stoppers out of the rum bottles they were carrying.

In May 1942 the Polish destroyer *Blyskawica* created a non-stop barrage of anti-aircraft fire in defence of Cowes and East Cowes. The destroyer had been built in 1935 in Cowes together with her sister ship. *Blyskawica* was in Cowes for refitting and if not for the ship's covering fire the damage to the town would have been far more extensive. There were eighty-two casualties that day, ten of whom died. However, 69 tons of bombs landed on the industrial area of Cowes resulting in considerable damage. The severity of the bombing of Cowes produced a similar exodus to that of Portsmouth with Cowes residents leaving on foot, bicycle or car for places not being intensively bombed.

After the Cowes raid German attacks were tip and run for the rest of 1942 and into the following year. On 7 July 1942 four bombs were dropped on the western Solent off Yarmouth that might have been directed at the assault craft preparing for the raid on Dieppe. A great deal of final planning for the raid took place at Cowes at HMS *Vectis* located at the Royal Yacht Squadron. As well as commandos who made up the bulk of the raiding force, training was also taking place on the island for those who had been recruited from the Territorials. A familiar sight was the Canadians stealing their way through hedgerows and gardens. Before they left they put on a party for the children of West Wight. On 14 July there was another attempt to knock out the pylons at the radar station with only slight damage being recorded. By Christmas, apart from unexploded bombs being washed up along its shoreline, the island was quieter and at Christmas and the New Year there was a blessed absence of sirens. However, in 1943 the Germans dropped another type of bomb, this time loaded not with high explosive but with Colorado beetles designed to destroy the island's potato crop that had doubled between 1939 and 1943. The Germans made the mistake of dropping them in groups of 50 or 100 clusters, so they could be easily found and eliminated. The island was nicknamed the Isle of Plenty because of its success in farming and horticulture. There were even razor blades, in short supply and rationed on the mainland, because these had been purchased in 1939 for the holiday trade that never happened. By the end of the war 214 islanders had been killed, 274 seriously wounded and more than 11,000 buildings destroyed.

The Isle of Wight had a mystery wrapped up as an enigma in the shape of Dorothy O'Grady. She had been sentenced to death for treason involved in collecting information about gun emplacements and defensive preparation in the early part of the war. This involved drawing detailed maps and recording details of the movement of troops on the island. However, those who knew her could not believe that the woman known as 'dotty Dorothy' and often seen walking her Labrador Rob could have been a spy. Much detailed information about her was a secret until 1995 when the full details of her case were revealed. In 1940 she was on her own because her husband, seventeen years her senior, had been called back into the fire service in London. It was her insistence on walking into prohibited areas that brought her to the attention of the police. In August they pressed charges against her for being in a prohibited area and she was summoned to appear at Ryde Magistrates' Court. She failed to appear and went on the run, finally being captured living under an assumed name in a boarding house at Totland Bay on the west coast of the island. The evidence the police had accumulated showed her activities in map-making, cutting telephone wires and wearing a swastika badge under the lapel of her coat. Following her trial at Winchester Crown Court she was sentenced to death for treason. However, because the jury had been misdirected by the judge this was reduced to fourteen years' imprisonment.

The declassified files in 1995 showed that the maps O'Grady had produced would have been of major use to a German invading force during Operation SEA LION, the planned invasion of Britain. However, there is no evidence that she made contact with the Germans and may have reasoned that should they invade she would be very much in favour with the Germans. After nine years in prison she was released and returned to the island where she died aged 85. This was not before she had given an interview to the *Daily Express* claiming that the whole thing had been a joke and that the sentence of death passed on her had been the greatest thrill of her life. In possession of an IQ of 140 (the average being 100), she described the intense excitement of going on trial for her life as making her feel like somebody. O'Grady's history was shown to involve forgery, theft and prostitution for which she had served prison sentences. Reports from the prison governor at Aylesbury Prison point to a highly disturbed woman who regularly self-harmed, which may solve some of the mystery surrounding O'Grady.

CHAPTER TWENTY-ONE

Lymington and Cove's Sacrifice

Nothing throws a stronger light on the demands made on small towns throughout Hampshire than the roll of honour of the dead in Lymington. The town had a close association with the sea, eighteen men giving their lives in the Royal Navy and four in the Merchant Navy. There were seventeen killed serving in the Royal Air Force and thirty-one became casualties while serving in the army.

Men such as Arthur Payne who worked at Wellworthy Engineering left his workbench to serve in the 19th Field Regiment and was killed in France in 1940. Herbert Ireland was a stoker on board HMS *Granville*. He was aged 26 when the ship was sunk on 19 January 1940. Geoffrey Charles was aged 24 and had worked at builders' merchants in the town when his ship was torpedoed in the North Sea on 18 February 1940. There were 15 survivors but 157 men were lost. Lieutenant Donald Pirie, DSC died when his submarine *Spearfish* was depth-charged on 2 August 1940. He had joined the Royal Navy as a Dartmouth cadet in 1927. On being promoted to sub-lieutenant he moved to serving in U-class submarines. In April 1939 he was posted as second-in-command of the submarine *Spearfish*. His submarine was sunk by German submarine *U-34*, there being only a single survivor. On 31 July *Spearfish* had sailed from Rosyth for patrols off the Norwegian coast. Leading Seaman Cyril Day was on HMS *Delight* when on 28 August 1940 she was attacked in Portland Harbour by enemy aircraft, resulting in his death at the age of 27. Edgar Brown was a quartermaster on HMS *Wilna* when she was attacked in the Channel, leading to his death at age 22. Ordinary Seaman Robert Dashwood was serving on HMS *Esk* when she was sunk by a mine in just two minutes, resulting in the deaths of 9 officers and 151 ratings on 1 September. He was 20 years old and had trained at HMS *Collingwood*. Robert came from a family that had a deep attachment to the sea. He was a member of the Lymington Rovers Football Club, which in September 1940 had fifty members serving in the forces and thirty enrolled for Home Defence. Peter Todd was a radio operator with the Merchant Navy. On 14 January 1943 his ship carrying aviation fuel was torpedoed. He was aged just 21. Ernest Haywood died when his ship, the *Canada Star*, was torpedoed in the Atlantic. He was 27. Robert Isted was serving on HMS *Vervain*, a Flower-class corvette, when she was torpedoed by U-boat *U-1276* on 20 January 1945 off the coast of Waterford, Ireland while escorting a convoy. He had joined the Royal

Navy at the beginning of the war and was aged 24. Lieutenant Robert Bygott disappeared with submarine HMS *P33* which sailed from Malta to intercept an Italian convoy. Nothing further was heard of the vessel, but it was assumed to have been sunk by depth-charge or by attack from an Italian torpedo boat. Robert was aged 21. Petty Officer Cyril Hurst was 30 – senior to the other men listed – and was married and setting up house in Portsmouth from which his wife and son, David, were bombed out. He had made a career for himself in the Royal Navy serving all over the world. His ship HMS *Limbourne* had been dispatched with HMS *Charybdis* to intercept a German convoy. The Germans made use of superior radar and sank both ships in October 1943. Forty were rescued from the *Limbourne* but Cyril was not among them. Able Seaman Fred Cassey was just 19 years old when he was killed on board HMS *Cassandra* when she was torpedoed by the German submarine *U-365* near Murmansk in Arctic Russia on 11 December 1944. At 14 he had left school to become a delivery boy for a local butcher's shop. At 16 he went to work at Wellworthys and enlisted for the Home Guard. At 18 he joined the Royal Navy and trained at Chatham. Peter Todd was second radio officer on board the Merchant Navy ship *British Dominion*. The vessel was a tanker carrying aviation fuel and sailed in a convoy from Trinidad that was attacked by a wolf pack of U-boats in mid-Atlantic. Of the nine tankers, only two reached their destination of Gibraltar. On 11 January 1943 Peter Todd went down with his ship when she was sunk by *U-620*. He was aged 21.

Cove is a suburb of Farnborough but even from such a small hamlet a great sacrifice was made. Some of these were Corporal Robert Fraser Wilson of the Gordon Highlanders who, after being a PoW following his capture at Dunkirk, died shortly after the end of the war in January 1946. Robert James Cook, originally of the Hampshires, was killed in Libya following his training on the Isle of Wight. Laurence Victor Chamberlain, who had worked at the RAE, lost his life when HMS *Exmouth* was sunk on 21 January 1940 when he was aged 22. Did *Exmouth* hit a mine or was she torpedoed? Royal Marine Richard John Baker was posted to HMS *Barham* with the role of manning the X-turret 15in gun. On 25 November 1941 *Barham* was hit when operating in convoy, resulting in the deaths of 862 men including the 19-year-old Richard. He is remembered on the Royal Navy Memorial at Southsea. John Albert Beale (Jack to his mates) originally joined the Hampshires before being attached to the Northamptonshire Regiment to fight in the Italian campaign, dying on 25 June 1944. Aubrey Harold Edwards, following pilot's training in Canada, flew with Bomber Command from Pocklington, Yorkshire, where after five months' service he was reported missing after a raid on Hamburg on the night of 8/9 April 1942. Douglas Albert Payne was on board HMS *Calcutta* when she was blown up in January 1942. There were always costly accidents associated with the preparation for campaigns. In the case of Sergeant David J. Owen's death, he was in a group of Royal Army

Engineers developing the flail mine-destroying tank. He was following in a tank behind the experimental vehicle when one of the real mines used for a demonstration failed to explode. His tank ran over the unexploded mine and he was killed. A leading stoker in the Royal Navy, Bertram Edward Seal was killed on HMS *Arrow* off Algiers on 4 August 1943. In the last days of the war Trooper Phillip C. Brown, aged 22, was killed on 14 April 1945 as his 1st Regiment Cheshires dashed across Germany to link up with the Russians on the Elbe. He was the last soldier of his unit to be killed in action. When the *Royal Oak* sank on 14 October 1939 Frank Ede, a leading stoker, went down with her. During the break-out of British troops in France from Normandy, Private John Woodman was killed on 30 July 1944. On Churchill's orders, details of the sinking of HMT *Lancastria* on 17 June 1940 were not reported. Perhaps he thought that the human mind can only cope with so much reality after Dunkirk. The death toll was 4,000, among them Ronald Arthur Silver, Royal Engineer from Cove who, finding escape from Dunkirk blocked, had gone to St Nazaire where he had boarded the ill-starred *Lancastria* along with fellow Royal Engineers.

CHAPTER TWENTY-TWO

Prisoners of War

He looked wild-eyed at them and was horrified when he recognized them as German troops. He was on his early-morning paper run and still sleepy but this was like a waking nightmare. Was this the invasion of Gosport with all that he had read about? Here they were in Gosport at 6.30 am. This is how one young man described the marching column of hundreds of German prisoners captured in Normandy. He was convinced that this was the first day of an invasion by the absence of any British soldiers. In fear of what was to come, he dropped his bike in front of the oncoming marchers only to see them divide and walk around his bike. Only belatedly did a few military policemen appear armed with Sten guns. One grinned at him as he passed. Then he became aware of the strange smell coming from the ranks of the passing men and he thought it must have been a strange cigarette they smoked. Later he realized it had resulted from the delousing to which the men had been subjected.

As the war continued, so did the number of Axis prisoners increase, particularly after the D-Day landings. At one time there were 250,000 PoWs in camps in Britain. In December an escape plan by Waffen SS officers in a Devizes camp to break out and seize arms and tanks was taken very seriously because most British troops were overseas. In contrast with the experience of Allied PoWs in Germany, the British authorities made considerable efforts to ensure that German prisoners were appropriately treated and enjoyed reasonable conditions. However, for observers among the civilian population, mainly women struggling to feed their families on extremely limited rations, this level of care seemed excessive. By 1945, when there were eye-witness reports of concentration camps in Germany, this feeling of undue privilege was further highlighted. In the final April of the war there was a shortage of potatoes which was blamed on the bad spring. However, a Portsmouth housewife writing from Eastney to the *Portsmouth Evening News* pointed to the drain on food supplies created by hundreds of German prisoners:

> Why not tell the people the truth and say we have thousands of Germans to feed? All the women in queues agree with me and say that the Germans should have potato peeling soup (and less), which they have been giving our men. We would gladly put out our peelings in swill buckets to be collected.

German PoWs arriving in Southampton.

A Fratton woman added: 'The potato peeling soup she speaks of is almost too good for them. Give them what they gave our prisoners and save decent food for decent English people to enjoy.' A third correspondent drew attention to German torture chambers and said that German prisoners were treated like 'fighting cocks' and were seen sunbathing in the midst of a bombed-out city. The matter was raised in Parliament and a plea that all prisoners were not necessarily Nazi torturers drew other angry responses.

By the end of the war most areas in Portsmouth had a PoW camp located close to them. Wounded German PoWs were housed at Queen Alexandra Hospital at Cosham, located in heavily-guarded Nissen huts, while on the western side of the harbour at Hardway German prisoners were arriving in batches of 600 to 800. At Forton barracks they were interrogated and deloused. Close by was a firing range which terrified the prisoners who thought they were going to be summarily shot. One watching 10-year-old had a swastika badge pinned on to him by a German soldier before the soldier was chased back into the marching column. Close to Aldershot was Anglesey House which was reserved for German prisoners working in the area, principally on farms. Setley Plain Camp 65 near Brockenhurst housed Italian prisoners from North Africa as well as Germans who worked locally. It had been set up in 1941 and every morning lorries could be seen taking prisoners to and from their work in the New Forest accompanied by a single guard with a rifle. They worked at Denny's Sawmill, Lyndhurst and in the gardens of local people in Brockenhurst. Following Italy's surrender in 1943 the Italian prisoners were labelled as 'cooperators' and moved out of the camp to be replaced by German prisoners after D-Day. German work camps were found at Fareham, Thedden Grange (294) near Alton, Haig Lines at Crookham, at Sway (Camp 645), Fargo Camp Larkhill (Camp 672), Oakhanger near Bordon and at Chandler's Ford. Camps such as Ossemsley, near New Milton, had previously held the 56th Infantry Brigade before D-Day. It featured triple barbed wire and squares of US tents in the holding area. A number were dotted around Aldershot such as Puckridge Camp, Willems barracks and Beaumont barracks. For prisoners arriving after D-Day, Camp C19 was set up as a temporary measure. High-risk prisoners were housed on the Isle of Wight at Osborne House, New Close, Beatrice Avenue and Whitwell.

At first fraternization with Axis prisoners was strictly forbidden but two years after the war on 14 August 1947 the first marriage between a PoW and a British woman took place. Heinz and June marked their 60th anniversary with their six children, twelve grandchildren and fifteen great-grandchildren. They spoke of the hostility they experienced in the early days of their relationship. Even by 1948 there were still 23,729 PoWs in 120 camps that remained open.

A German general taken prisoner and arriving in Hampshire.

Hampshire PoWs in Germany.

CHAPTER TWENTY-THREE

Hampshire and D-Day

The experience of defeat in 1940 in France and the failure of the Dieppe raid had resulted in Churchill having grave doubts of the likely success of any attempt by Allied forces to successfully attack the European mainland. From 1942 Stalin had been calling for a second front and Roosevelt began to echo this call. In Hampshire towns local newspapers were calling for the second front to come to the assistance of the beleaguered Russians. Churchill's response was to promote campaigns in North Africa, Sicily and Italy, claiming that they represented Hitler's soft underbelly. Stalin and Roosevelt grew increasingly frustrated as resources of men were channelled to these campaigns and not towards a second-front invasion of France but the expectation that it would happen in 1943 was effectively frustrated by Churchill. However, reluctantly he had to agree that detailed planning for an invasion of France had to begin and Hampshire became the major focus for planning Operation OVERLORD as it would be code-named.

Much would depend on the mobilization of the immense resources of the United States towards Operation OVERLORD. British morale had been fortified through victory at El Alamein in 1942 after a whole series of defeats and retreats by British armed forces. At the conference of Allied leaders at Casablanca in early 1943 a target date in the summer of 1944 was agreed upon. At the same time it was recognized that the harbours of Kent were not adequate to accommodate a force of this scale and the Solent was agreed upon. In the summer of 1943 an advanced American unit Headquarters 14th Port arrived in Southampton to assist with the handling of the huge amount of matériel that was to flood in. It should be remembered that pre-war Southampton had been largely a passenger port and the first task was to bring in cranes capable of dealing with war matériel on this scale. There was immediate competition for space because the Admiralty had already begun the process of constructing landing craft and construction projects to support the invasion.

Where did the term D-Day come from? It has come to only have reference to the day on which military landings at Normandy commenced, with the day before being termed D-1. The term H-hour is used for the actual time when action would begin. Code names around the planning and organization of D-Day were employed for specific military operations. OVERLORD was used for the invasion of north-west Europe. The actual assault on the beaches

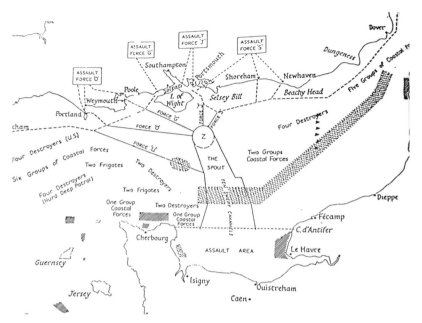

Map of D-Day invasion plans.

was referred to as Operation NEPTUNE. It began on 6 June and finished on 30 June. By that time the Allies had established a foothold in Normandy with Operation OVERLORD taking the Allies over the River Seine on 19 August 1944 and the Battle of Normandy is seen as concluding when the Allies entered Paris on 25 August. Involved in the Allied forces were troops from Australia, Belgium, Czechoslovakia, France, Greece, The Netherlands, New Zealand, Norway and Poland. On 6 June 156,000 troops landed including 73,000 Americans: 23,250 on UTAH Beach, 34,250 on OMAHA Beach and 15,500 airborne troops. In the British and Canadian sector 83,115 were landed (61,715 of them British): 24,970 on GOLD Beach, 21,400 on JUNO Beach, 28,845 on SWORD Beach and 7,900 airborne troops. There were 11,590 aircraft available to support the landings flying 14,674 sorties. Of these, 127 were lost. Operation NEPTUNE, the code-name of the naval contribution, included 7,839 vessels comprising 2,113 naval combat craft, 4,126 landing ships/craft, 736 ancillary craft and 864 merchant ships. By the end of June (D+25), 326,367 troops, 54,186 vehicles and 104,428 tons of supplies had been landed. Casualties for D-Day have been estimated at 10,245 including 2,700 British, 945 Canadians, and 6,600 Americans. In all, 425,000 Allied and German troops were killed, wounded or went missing during the Battle of Normandy, which also saw the loss of 24 warships and 35 merchantmen.

After Dunkirk in 1940, the British army consisted of 37 equipped divisions in comparison with the Germans' 250 divisions. With the German attack on the Soviet Union and the removal of fears of invasion, discussion began about a return to France. It quickly became apparent that any landing in France would have to involve a joint operation of army, navy and Air Force. The disastrous raid on Dieppe clearly indicated that as with Gallipoli in the First World War new thinking and development would have to take place before there could be any chance of success. Further, as this was the beginning of a campaign to defeat Germany, systems to supply an army to achieve this would have to be put in place. In order to do this, effective harbours capable of landing huge quantities of resources would have to be employed. Unfortunately the options available on the north-western French coast were limited and would inevitably be heavily fortified. Such an army would devour millions of tons of oil in achieving victory. PLUTO (the pipeline under the ocean) was a scheme designed to avoid the obvious hazard of transporting oil and petrol by tankers. Experiments began to design pipes capable of allowing oil to move down a pipeline under the sea. The scheme was designed by Arthur Hartley, chief engineer with Anglo Iranian Oil. Tests took place on the pipeline, running it from the mainland to the Isle of Wight that became a terminal for the oil which was then pumped to France. By 12 August 172 million gallons were pumped between then and May 1945.

Hayling Island played a very important role in developing the landing craft necessary for Operation OVERLORD. It was discovered that the island's beaches were similar in constitution to those in Normandy. A vital advantage was that the holiday camps, so much a feature of Hayling Island, could provide vital accommodation for the 60,000 workers required for landing-boat construction. A major change was that the Royal Marines would now command landing craft. They played an active part in the training taking place on both sides of Chichester harbour. Much of the private housing on the island was requisitioned for military use. Mr R.A. Beachill from Copnor, an electrical engineer, thought that the soldiers were being 'psyched up' for D-Day. Mr Beachill had become an electrical apprentice on leaving school in January 1944. There were gas alerts when everyone had to put on gas masks. Ancillary workers had to be accompanied by armed guards following them like shadows. He recalls seeing both Montgomery and Eisenhower at close quarters when they addressed the assembling troops. On 3 June the lorry to take them to the camp where they were working arrived but the camp was completely deserted.

Perhaps the greatest feat was the construction of the Mulberry harbours which essentially underpinned the whole invasion on 6 June. The idea had been advocated by Churchill in the Great War involving a landing stage that floated in the sea. Why were they called Mulberry? In the summer of 1942 the Supreme Headquarters of the Applied Expeditionary Force (SHAEF) group had begun considering what would be involved in constructing an artificial harbour. The question arose about what name was going to be attached to it. As it was a hot day they had moved out into the garden. 'Well,' said one of the assistants working with the group, 'why not call it Mulberry because we are enjoying the shade of a mulberry bush?'

The plan was to build two artificial harbours based on giant phoenixes of 60ft in height. At first experiments were carried out using balloons to provide buoyancy for the harbours but this was recognized as being vulnerable to shrapnel. Measuring 200ft long and 25ft high, they would each weigh at least 1,000 tons. The concept was that the docks would ebb and flow with the movement of the tide. They were to be built in Stokes Bay, Portsmouth and would involve 1,600 skilled men. Where were men with the skills involved in scaffolding, steel bending and steel erection? However, a Liverpool firm was identified with some of the skills needed for the building of concrete structures the size of five-storey houses. Building required 3,000 tons of concrete each day for a construction that was larger than the docks in Dover. Caissons were to act as a pier head and most of the dry docks in Portsmouth were requisitioned for their construction from mid-1943. The huge constructs were built one behind each other on a keel block wall 20ft high that had to be hauled from the dry dock to a reinforced shoreline. Inside the caissons were places allocated for the crew who would sink them into place on the Normandy beaches. The largest had a displacement of 6,044 tons. The 15 pier heads built with 212 caissons at Gosport were transferred across the Solent to be submerged until they were resurrected immediately prior to D-Day. Some 1,600 labourers worked on them as scaffolders, carpenters and steel-benders, each working a twelve-hour day.

They were to prove effective in creating calm water inside the harbour made up of 'gooseberries' of block ships. Unfortunately the worst storm in thirty years destroyed the Mulberry on the American landing beach but the one off the British beach was repaired and played a valuable role in facilitating supplies for the invasion. Disaster struck when the first caissons being manoeuvred towards the water collapsed, killing three workmen. Behind the caissons were bombardons intended to act as a breakwater and the whole construction was to be bolstered by fifty-three block ships. These were obsolete naval vessels. There would be roadways on top of the construction called 'whales'. The whole of the country was scoured for tug boats required to tow the caissons to the storage space allocated for them. At one time 45,000 men were working on the Mulberry project. Finding accommodation for these men was difficult with all hostel space in Portsmouth occupied and only tented accommodation available. A special boat called a Slug had to be constructed to work beneath a Mulberry to secure its various parts together. Security was so tight in Gosport that moving within the town sometimes created difficulties. Mr Beachill's first job was working on the caissons on

Hayling Beach and he worked on temporary power supply for the project. He remembered the extremely hard-working Irishmen who were employed throughout the extremely cold January and February of 1944 with little shelter being provided. The men were billeted in one of the island's holiday camps. Frantic efforts were made to launch the four caissons they were working on because several of the compartments were flooded with water. Mrs Grace Townsend, living close by, recalled that the launch of the caissons was seen by residents as a major event. Captain Alex J. Wale from Gosport worked on the 30th Supply and Repair flotilla of landing barges forming up in Langstone Harbour in early 1944 and left from there for Normandy on 5 June. The barges were Thames lighters with engines and provision made for personnel. He was part of the SWORD force with the task of supporting smaller landing craft. Marine Turner from Hayling Island was on LCI (Landing Craft, Infantry) (G), one of eighty-six large landing craft when it sailed from Langstone Harbour on 5 June. As one of the larger landing craft it would unload directly on to the beach. It also possessed guns to be fired in support of the landing troops. With his crew of thirty he reached his beach at 4.00 am. Peter Bird on the 1st LBV (Landing Barge Vehicle) loaded 70 to 80 tons of stores in Southampton in May, meaning that when navigating the heavy seas of 6 June water poured into the boat because it had only 18in of freeboard. Throughout the voyage they had to man the ship's pumps to keep it afloat. They managed to fend

Huge concrete caissons being built as part of a Mulberry harbour.

off a mine with a boat hook. Of his flotilla of twelve, only nine reached a Normandy beach. Bob Miles had trained at HMS *Northney* in the skills required for beaching and kedging landing craft and he played a key part in the landings.

From the experimental work associated with D-Day came the Bailey bridge, recognized all over the world. The designer of the bridge was Sir Donald Bailey who had developed the bridge at the Experimental Bridging Establishment at Christchurch and had created a pre-fabricated mobile construction in sections 10ft long by 5ft high by 12ft wide, with crossing steel panels joined with high-tensile steel pins top and bottom. His construction was capable of carrying 40-ton tanks and 100-ton railway trains. By 1945, 3,000 Bailey bridges had been constructed. Even Europe's greatest rivers were no match for the utility of the Bailey bridge.

The first acute issue to be dealt with was who was going to be in overall command of Operation OVERLORD? Clearly because of the dominant contribution the Americans would be making it should be a US general. At first General Marshall was proposed, but Roosevelt insisted on him remaining in Washington. The next in line was Dwight D. Eisenhower who arrived to begin establishing his headquarters at Southwick House near Portsmouth. British and Commonwealth troops would be led by Bernard Montgomery whose caravan duly arrived and was located in the grounds of Southwick House and became the focus for D-Day activity from April 1944. The identification of where the huge concentration of troops and resources would be located relating to where the landings in Normandy would take place had to be determined. The British landings at SWORD, GOLD and JUNO beaches were closest to the Hampshire coast with not only major harbours like the Solent but also the inlets and coves where many of the 7,000 vessels required could be moored and effectively hidden from the Germans. Apart from General Patton whose headquarters were not at Southwick and who advocated a landing at Pas-de-Calais, agreement was reached that the landing should take place on the Normandy beaches. The American beaches OMAHA and UTAH meant that the concentration of some of their troops would be based further west in Dorset. From December 1943 the vast logistical task of putting an invasion force together began, faced with the difficulty of finding skilled labour. It was quickly realized that the crux of the whole operation was to create a bridgehead in a lodgement area that would be superior to any sent to dislodge them. Admiral Bertram Ramsay would have a force of almost 7,000 vessels including 4,000 ships and landing craft, 1,200 naval vessels, 736 ancillary craft and 836 merchant supply vessels. Air Chief Marshal Leigh-Mallory had 11,500 aircraft available to protect the troops from aerial attack, many of whom would fly from Hampshire airfields.

For an invasion on this scale, Hampshire offered a large number of advantages. Southern Rail at this time had a network (see map, page ii) promoting access to the crucial south-coast launch areas for 6 June 1944. By D-Day there had been 31,136 special trains carrying men and materials to their jumping-off point in the run-up to departure reaching 1,415 a week. To facilitate this, increased work had to take place on sidings, the track, sheds and platforms. Extended platforms had to be built at Micheldever, an American base, with a 460ft extension, together with a down and up loop for 70m wagons capable of handling seventy wagons at Romsey, six new sidings at Brockenhurst and sidings at Fareham, Havant and Chandler's Ford. Rail was an essential factor in the supply of material for the armaments factory at Priddy's Hard. Work on adapting rolling stock to carry tanks and military vehicles took place at the railway workshops at Eastleigh and an area to the north of Eastleigh was designated as a major marshalling centre for troops, while Brockenhurst became a major storage place for bombs. Dunbridge had 15 miles of sidings and 154 covered sheds. The Royal Dockyard proved not only capable of building landing craft but also offering repair facilities for the merchant ships and mine-sweepers that were to play a crucial role. HMS *Clarence* in Portsmouth provided a vital victualling service, not only for the landed troops but also for the troops assembled prior to D-Day. Every day 20,000 tons of fresh water had to be distributed along with 33,000lb of bread, 400 tons of potatoes and 100 tons of meat. For the Southern Command based in Aldershot, Southampton was the traditional gateway to Europe for an invasion force of this kind. It was becoming apparent that women working in the war-related industries around Eastleigh, Southampton, Gosport and Portsmouth were more than capable of replacing men in the process of making Hampshire the largest military base in the world. A women's labour force of 1,700 was employed in factories at Shoreham, Exbury, Marchwood and Lymington. All of this activity highlighted an acute shortage of labour and the security problem involved in the employment of labourers drawn from neutral Ireland. This was only partially solved by the recruitment of men who had recently been conscripted and were awaiting assignment to the armed forces.

The lessons of Gallipoli and Dieppe proved that there was a need for purpose-built landing craft capable of putting troops ashore on an open beach. The decision to land at low water in order to surprise the Germans meant that a special type of flat-bottomed self-propelled vessel would have to be produced. Contracts were given to ship-building firms in the area to construct landing craft to this specification and to include hard landing craft for tanks being tested on slipways around the Solent. Because of the thousands of troops assembling in Southampton and Portsmouth, power and water shortages began to develop. As previously described, temporary airfields were created to support D-Day.

Packed into the Solent, so closely that it was possible to walk from the Isle of Wight to the mainland in the days prior to D-Day, were some of the 1,300 warships involved and some of the major battleships, 221 smaller combat vessels, 1,000 mine-sweepers that were required to sweep passages for the invasion, 800 merchant ships and 60 block ships as well as 30 other assorted boats. In the air, the Air Force had sent 11,000 fighters and bombers to support the invasion. On 6 June, 156,000 troops were successfully landed. The death toll for the landing on all five beaches was 8,975.

Among the range of technical expertise called into question by OVERLORD was that of weather-forecasting. At the end of April the SHAEF group had to give serious consideration to the weather for 6 June. Group Captain James Stagg, a Royal Air Force weather expert, was asked for his advice on what was a warm summer day. Unfortunately there was a serious storm seen in the three-day survey on 3 June in the forecast for the D-Day landings. After Eisenhower heard this, he called for a vote among the SHAEF group as to whether the invasion should go ahead. The decision at Southwick House was to delay, despite the risk this might impose on the desperately-created secrecy surrounding OVERLORD. (A whole shadow invasion force had been placed near Dover to give the Germans a false indication that the attack would be made on Pas-de-Calais.) Stagg returned to a late reconvened meeting to announce that there was a small window of opportunity on 6 June. Despite the fact that the sea was very rough as a result of the storm on the previous day, the invasion went ahead.

In the Aldershot Command tanks were being tested for their water resistance on Hawley Lake. The narrow roads of Aldershot, Farnborough and Fleet were proving a problem and their surfaces were being torn up by the tanks' tracks. In Exercise Kate, the Canadians began testing their equipment for a passage across the Seine. In the days leading up to D-Day Queen's Drive was packed with tanks and other military hardware. Under the town's chestnut trees were trucks, motor-cycles, bicycles and stores. The Hog's Back (nearby in Surrey) was bumper-to-bumper with tanks and military vehicles. One story has it that the Canadians had buried stores on the heathland around Aldershot in the hope of returning to sell it after the war.

Viewed from Gosport, people were not aware that D-Day was happening around them but there was a consciousness of a build-up towards a big operation and that the town would be closely involved. As a town bounded on three sides by the sea, it overlooked Portsmouth Harbour and Spithead. It was able to offer an anchorage for craft of all kinds as well as storage space for supplies. It provided an embarkation point at Hardway and walkways were built out from the beach to assist the loading of tanks and military vehicles at Beach Street and Stokes Bay. Stokes Bay proved itself to be an excellent versatile point of embarkation. Advantage was taken of the work in beach-hardening that had begun in 1943. This was done by the use of pre-cast concrete slabs. There had to be work to enable tanks to traverse the town. In the two or three days immediately prior to the embarkation of OVERLORD forces, even the pavements were taken up for the storage of oil drums and a special pass was required to travel from Portsmouth to Gosport. On Priddy's Hard, 20,000 tons of ammunition were loaded along with 50,000 rockets that were to be fired from specially-adapted craft. A ship carrying a smoke-making machine blew up in the period immediately prior to D-Day.

Materials were being delivered to Gosport stores' centres. Local people invited soldiers into their houses for meals. Many were billeted at Fort Brockhurst and then a week after the invasion hundreds of prisoners began to arrive. An order not to fraternize with the soldiers was disregarded. Mr Mitzen spoke of volunteers going to Hardway to assist in carrying the wounded from the hospital ships. He mentioned many that had lost arms and legs and were in a terrible condition.

In the factories people were working twelve-hour days at lathes and on repair equipment, cleaning gun parts, repairing cartridges, spray-painting, soldering and putting equipment together. Ann Joseph was able to observe from her home in Havant the whole move towards D-Day coming from Southwick House and moving towards Portsdown, feeling that as a civilian she was stuck on the northern side of the hill while the military took the southern side. They could observe soldiers practising rock-climbing at Portsdown's chalk pits. 'On the evening of 5 June we heard more than the usual number of planes and then Langstone Harbour was suddenly empty.' Another feature of D-Day was the return of evacuees. Edmond Kean was working as a chip boy providing fish and chips to the assembled troops in Southampton. He was awoken on the night of embarkation by an intense roar of tanks starting up for their move to departure. As the troops moved to their embarkation points in places like The Avenue, it was as if the hopes and aspirations of the whole country went with them. 'As we passed through Southampton its people gave us a wonderful welcome. Each time we halted we were plied with cups of tea and cake, much to the consternation of the Military Police. We had strict orders about fraternisation between civilians and soldiers.' Maureen Jones was working in the vast plotting room in Southwick House at 1.00 pm on 6 June when the news came through that HMS *Arethusa*, the ship on which her brother was serving, had suffered a direct hit. Fortunately he was not among the casualties. 'If you started thinking of the thousands of men who would be killed you wouldn't have been able to do your job.'

Commanding LCI(S) 516 with a crew that had overseen sea training was one of New Zealand's foremost poets, Denis Glover. He took Lord Lovat's 6th Commando Brigade 2 Troop under Lieutenant Colonel Mills-Roberts to Ouistreham and was awarded a DSC for the bravery he displayed on 6 June. He and his crew rescued the crew of the 233rd Warwickshire Battalion (Birmingham) from the sinking LCI(L) 130 and later some of the crew of LCI(S) 517. Glover and other commanders on the landing boats were careful that there was ammunition available for their guns, having learned the lesson of Dieppe where ammunition was sent on separate vessels. Haslar Hospital in

Portsmouth was made available for the wounded from OVERLORD boosted by advanced dressing stations at Queen Alexandra Barracks and naval sick bays. A blood bank was set up at Portsmouth Grammar School. Then Portsmouth Harbour was emptier than at any time during the war. Buses began to run along the front for the first time in years. There was an expectation that there would be some sort of retaliation from the Germans but it just did not come. Then the first ambulance arrived with the wounded. An observer at St James's Hospital remembers that the first wounded were Canadians. He was responsible for getting details of next of kin and to write on the patients' behalf to their relatives saying that they were safe. He saw some terrible injuries and said that nearly all of them were totally black with dirt. The very young were shy and embarrassed when asked about girlfriends to whom they could write. At the moment of public rejoicing about D-Day, there was the private grief of someone in Portsmouth who had then lost two brothers. One had been lost in the Spanish Civil War and the other on the beaches of Normandy.

A fascinating insider's picture of how D-Day unfolded is given by Lieutenant Commander George Honour who was the commander of a new prototype submarine *X23* and was positioned just off SWORD Beach with a crew of five. They loaded with supplies at HMS *Dolphin* a few days before D-Day as part of a two-submarine activity with *X20*. They were towed out of Portsmouth Harbour to a position just off the Isle of Wight and cast off. At 3 knots per hour, it took them from Friday night to Sunday morning to reach SWORD Beach. Their role was to guide the first landing craft into the appropriate beach. Unfortunately because of stormy weather the planned landing on 5 June was postponed by a day until 4.30 the following morning. At 6.00 am they saw a mass of ships making up the invasion fleet and with their periscope observed German staff cars racing along the front. For the next two hours the commander had a grandstand view of the invasion. Unfortunately the ship meant to take them in tow had gone to the wrong beach but ultimately they met up and on their return received a heroes' welcome.

Stanley Roy Nash from Tadley, near Basingstoke, remembers events around his war and D-Day. He was one of four brothers. One of his older brothers was called up for the BEF in the early part of the war and was safely evacuated from Dunkirk. One brother became a cook and another, who was a year older, went to France on D-Day with the Royal Engineers. Roy was called up in 1943 and went to Colchester for training with the Royal Berkshires. Shortly before D-Day he was called to the guard room to be told that he was too young to be part of the invasion force. This proved to be only a short let-off for within days he had to choose a regiment to join because his 5th Battalion had been so badly mauled in the landing that it had ceased to exist. He chose the 11th Armoured Division of the Monmouthshires. However, Roy was wounded on 2 April 1945 and flown back to Park Prewett Hospital where he was operated on by Sir Harold Gillies.

Maureen Bolster, working on HMS *Tormentor* at Southampton, on 1 May 1944 felt the long-awaited invasion of France was about to happen. She wrote to her fiancé Francis Earle Wells who was serving in North Africa:

> The first of May. It can't be long now. My country is on the verge of its greatest campaign of all time. It's too immense. It's too shattering. I hardly dare to think what it will mean, the lives lost and the number of everything involved – ships, planes, armour, men. One waits impatiently, waiting to get the strain of waiting over yet dreading it.

In May, Sylvia Key was working at Eisenhower's private switchboard (referred to as the 'red board'). She had been taken by truck to work under Cosham Forest. At Fort Southwick, Mary Macleod worked in an underground cavern typing out invasion plans in triplicate with two options: go ahead or delay. Firemen were seen in Southampton guarding ammunition dumps. Maureen Bolster confessed bursting into tears at the sight of very young men on a soccer field preparing for invasion. On the Isle of Wight Rozelle Rayner, who was working as a stoker, was called out on 4 June to rescue a landing craft that had broken down on Solent Water.

Monica Littleboy, viewing the vast D-Day armada, said:

> All day the ships went by with never a stop and not more than 100 yards between each vessel…this was no exercise. The cold choppy sea and the strong wind that was blowing almost seemed as though it would tear the little barrage balloons away. There were tugs and tankers, masses of them, landing craft of every kind, all towing one another bouncing about like peas in a drum. We could see the boats loaded with tanks and trucks very low in the water. Then came the troop ships dwarfing everything else, solid. We knew on board them were the Canadian men whom we had danced with at parties at the houses on the island. They were our personal friends.

Monica had little time to muse on this for within twenty-four hours casualties started to arrive on the Isle of Wight, often in transit to mainland hospitals. 'They were unloaded at Yarmouth and we raced up and down unloading patients and then reloading them onto hospital ships. I saw sights which I hope I may, please God, never see again,' said Monica. The men she accompanied on stretchers from the Isle of Wight were

> burned so badly as to be unrecognisable, only those with burning eyes could see us as we loaded our stretchers. I could feel the eyes following me as I tried to guide them around the ward. My smile was stiff and I felt full of sorrow for them. Something inside me was horror struck.

Maureen Bolster was appalled when she treated a young man so shellshocked that he could barely speak. 'Make me forget it, please make me forget it,' he said.

Montgomery in Portsmouth in January 1944 making plans for D-Day.

Troops in the New Forest waiting for D-Day.

In the New Forest loading supplies for D-Day troops.

Part of a Mulberry harbour structure with Bren gun.

Landing craft alongside wharves.

Jeeps and supplies awaiting loading for D-Day.

Landing craft alongside moorings ready for D-Day.

Training on a special gun prior to D-Day.

Hampshire Fire and Rescue Service supporting the waiting force for D-Day.

Train being loaded in readiness for part of action in France.

Landing craft loaded with cargo prior to D-Day.

On parade through the centre of Aldershot.

GIs training prior to D-Day.

German prisoners arriving after D-Day.

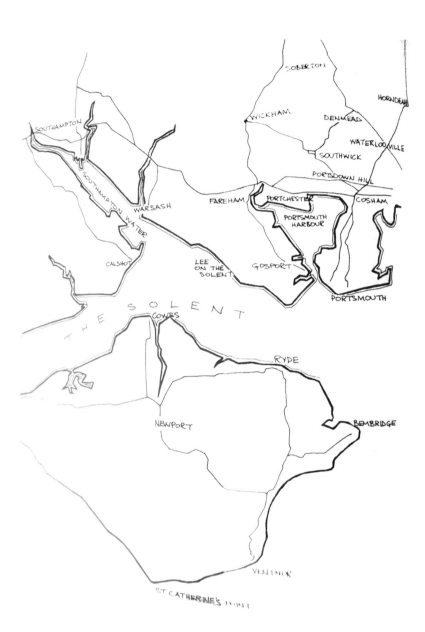

A map of the crucial Solent area.

Building the Mulberry harbour.

View of caisson awaiting transport to France as part of a Mulberry harbour.

CHAPTER TWENTY-FOUR

Carrying On Until the End

The people of Hampshire were granted a brief period to take stock after D-Day, disturbed only by V-1 and later V-2 weapons. There were eighty V-1s or doodlebugs that fell on Hampshire; a smaller number than the 2,304 that fell on London but bad enough for those who were killed or wounded. Coupled to this was the feeling of exhaustion from a population that had made such a contribution to the war effort after more than four years of total war. Two V-1s fell in the Aldershot and Farnborough area causing damage to 2,000 properties. In Chandler's Ford several others hit the town, one killing two members of a family in Pine Road. They also landed in Bitterne, Southampton, but no one was killed. In Portsmouth, Betty Kendrick remembered V-1 rockets falling on the town: 'Its engine would stop, followed by silence until the sound of the explosion.' The V-1 was a terror weapon that was sent diving towards humanity in Southampton from 3,000ft. Brian Martin and his 6-year-old brother Ray were in an Anderson shelter built by their father in the garden of their house. Their mother Gladys was with them when the V-1 landed just 6ft away:

> I was only six but can still recall being woken up by a huge noise at around 1 am. We were probably saved by a blast wall made up of old rabbit hutches filled with earth put up by my grandfather the day before. But they had been blown across the entrance of the shelter. Neighbours came to help dig us out.

Brian considered they were very lucky because although the bombing had almost stopped they had continued to use the shelter. With more V-1s beginning to target Southampton on 12 July there was a fear that the city was about to undergo another blitz but in reality the Germans' main target was London. When the 'all-clear' sounded on 5 November it marked the last bombing that Southampton had to endure.

Southampton was now dominated by great convoys of trains carrying 222,000 wounded men back from France and by the PoW transit camp located on the docks holding 185,000 internees. In September the blackout restrictions were lifted on all but a small number of coastal areas and the Home Guard held their standing-down parades. The WRNS who had been ships' mechanics, chart-correctors, confidential book officers, boarding

Women members of the armed forces parade in Aldershot. Salute to Soldiers' Week, July 1944.

officers, meteorologists, parachute-packers, signallers, coding officers, dispatch riders and motor transport riders, sometimes working forty-eight-hour shifts, had reached the zenith of their contribution. At HMS *Vectis* the WRNS were dealing with more than 100 ships per day. At HMS *Marshal Soult*, the minesweepers' depot in the Portsmouth Command, the WRNS had played a major role. Proof that the navy also sailed on its stomach was the 800 meals served every twenty-four hours at Combined Headquarters and the WRNS' mess cooking and serving 1,200 meals. From March 1945 married women began to be released from their posts with some occupational groups being declared redundant. Others were categorized in July as being obsolete. However, unlike at the end of the Great War, the whole of the WRNS was not disbanded but moves were made to turn it into a continuing professional service. At its peak there were 16,500 officers and men in barracks all over the Portsmouth area. In September 1945 Whale Island consisted of 150 officers, 215 gunnery instructors and 50 experimental officers, supported by 15 WRNS officers and 750 WRNS ratings. On 1 June demobilization commenced. Ships were returning to Portsmouth where most of them were laid up in any available creek or harbour. Some – like *Nelson*, the flagship of the Home Fleet – went to Portland where they were used for training purposes.

On 19 August 1944 Pilot Officer James Kingston Stellin of the Royal New Zealand Air Force, one of several thousand New Zealanders flying with the RAF over France, died when his plane crashed at St Maclou la Brière in France. Pilot Stellin is honoured in the small village with a population of 370 because as his plane went into a spiral he stayed in the cockpit in order to avoid crashing into the centre of the village. On 3 June 1944 he and three other Kiwi pilots had been posted to 609 Squadron of the RAF at Thorney Island airfield. During D-Day and after, they had flown numerous missions in support of the Allied invasion, attacking German tank concentrations on an almost daily basis. On 18 August 609 Squadron of Hawker Typhoons had destroyed at least seven tanks and twelve other vehicles. Stellin had followed this up by going out in the evening and attacking vehicles on the Vimoutiers to Orbec Road and setting five of them alight. A teacher from the village described what happened when Stellin was killed the following day:

> It was 10 o'clock in the morning when the sounds of an aircraft in difficulties first made us look up. The plane was 1,500 to 2,000 feet up and rapidly losing height. Suddenly realizing the great damage his plane would cause if it were to crash in the centre of the village the pilot straightened the plane with a vigorous and supreme effort, made a sharp climb, and then turning at a sharp angle it fell rapidly, crashing less than a mile away.

At the last moment Stellin tried to bail out but his parachute failed to open. He was 22 years old and his funeral in the village was attended by 1,200 people. In 1947 he was posthumously awarded the Croix de Guerre avec Palme.

Following many Hampshire-based squadrons move to France, in the wake of D-Day change was taking place. Up until July 1944 the 401st, 402nd and 485th Squadrons of the 370th Fighter Group of the Ninth Air Force of the USAAF flying Lockheed P-38 Lightning aircraft operated out of Andover airfield. They bombed radar installations, flak towers and escorted bombers attacking bridges and marshalling yards in France. The USAAF lost thirty-one P-38s prior to moving to France. Between 9 December 1944 and 5 March 1945, three Canadian Army Air Observation Squadrons were formed at RAF Andover. The pilots and observers had been recruited from the Royal Canadian Artillery and the Royal Canadian Air Force. RAF Andover guaranteed itself a place in history by becoming the first British military unit equipped to fly helicopters and by the formation of a training school for helicopter pilots in January 1945 under Squadron Leader B H Arkell.

Fund-raising to support the war effort and the production of planes representing the towns and cities of Hampshire continued. From 1943 the pace of experimentation and development in aviation stepped up at the RAE Farnborough. For Churchill, a special pressure compartment enabling him to fly at any altitude was designed so that he would not have to use an oxygen mask. As early as May 1943 Frank Whittle was beginning work on a Whittle W2B engine with 800lb of thrust. As a result of tests, a complete analysis of a turbine engine was achieved for the first time. High-speed dives were used in addition to experimental work in the wind tunnel. Although he survived having to bail out at 36,000ft while testing a jet engine, Flight Lieutenant Davie was killed on 4 January 1944 when the Meteor (Gloster F9/40) he was flying had one of its F2 engines disintegrate. On 23 March 1944 the decision was made to set up a National Experimental Establishment for aircraft development and design. A 5-mile runway was considered necessary, which should be located in Bedford. On 21 July twelve large packing cases arrived at the RAE in a Halifax with 12 tons of pieces from German guided missiles that had disintegrated during tests over Sweden. This was the first acquaintance with V-2 rockets confronting the RAE with the task of assembling the missile and attempting to analyse its design and performance. In July further parts of the V-1 were in the hands of the RAE and requiring analysis. By the end of 1944 the flying time of the RAE on new aeronautical developments amounted to 8,593 hours. As German aeronautical sites were overrun, the developmental work of German engineers and technicians became available and by the end of the war were under scrutiny at the RAE. Advances were made during 1945 in aviation medicine. At its peak around 6,000 personnel were employed during the war at the RAE. Located at Hartford Airfield, 264 Squadron was given the task of interfering with high-flying German reconnaissance planes over the Isle of Wight. Perhaps proof of their effectiveness was the lack of German awareness of the build-up towards D-Day throughout Hampshire. Dutch airmen flying fast Spitfires were able to offer some protection against V-1s. Meanwhile, the WVS continued to knit socks and gloves for servicemen, and collections of aluminium continued along with the collection of other recyclable materials.

The winter of 1944–45 was the cruellest of the war, not just because of the severity of the weather but also the ever-present shortages of almost everything. In October in Southampton the Americans introduced American football. Unfortunately in some areas there was a large increase in road accidents. Women appeared in court charged with soliciting around train and bus stations and being found in restricted areas. Clashes occurred in Southampton between the segregated black and white regiments of the US army, sometimes with local men joining in on the side of black servicemen. However, a harsher reality was the desperate housing shortage in parts of Hampshire that had been heavily bombed. In a desperate move to replace the hundreds of homes destroyed, prefabricated houses were hastily erected in Portsmouth. In the Highbury estate of Cosham, 100 bungalows of wooden waterproofed board were built, alongside 260 three-bedroomed houses on the Paulsgrave estate. Horror stories were emerging such as the former First World War sergeant and his family having to sleep in a chicken shed. Homeless families were forced to squat and even a petty officer's family in Fareham consisting of a wife and two children under the age of 2 was found sharing a house with two other families. A group calling themselves the Vigilantes was encouraging squatters to occupy empty houses. Faced with this, Portsmouth Council was given the right to requisition houses such as some of those in Southsea that had been empty for five years. Plans to rebuild parts of Portsmouth blitzed earlier in the war such as the Guildford Centre were developed, together with the Southsea shopping centre. Planners were advocating the construction of satellite towns outside previously overcrowded suburbs. Great shortages were still a fact of life with the population reconciled to massive queues. However, a housewife observed that 'Things are worse in Berlin.' In Portsdown a great motor garage was taken over to handle the process of demobilization of sailors from the navy when men received their regulation suits to begin their civilian life. With the barbed wire being removed from beaches, day-trippers began to appear on the beaches of Hayling Island and Southsea. When Belsen was reached by British forces, the true obscenity of what the war had been fought for was revealed by the skeletal refugees who arrived in Bishop's Waltham where a reception centre was established.

The coming of the New Year in 1945 was a bitterly cold one with shortages of coal and a constant fear of V-1 bomb attacks. Homes were without heating. At Portsbridge icebergs were observed in the sea. Coal merchants were weeks behind with deliveries as workers fell ill or were drafted into the armed forces. In desperation, the coal dump on Southsea Common was opened for families to collect their own coal. Women lined up with prams and boys pushed sledges to collect the precious cargo. However, for the first time in many years New Year 1945 was greeted with locomotive whistles, church bells in Portsmouth Cathedral ringing out for the first time since 1938 and factory sirens. For 500 Portsmouth children there was a special treat at Hilsea provided by American troops involving sweets, biscuits and the highly-prized candy bars that GIs had saved from their rations. Danger was never far away, however, as shown by the crashing of a plane at Horndean on a house where four children were sleeping and cutting the parish hall in half. These children had a lucky escape, revealed by the great hole in the ceiling above their heads. Portsmouth, considering the future, returned to its argument in favour of the construction of a large aircraft terminal for amphibious aircraft at Langstone but the argument was as unsuccessful as it had been in pre-war years.

At this point in the war it was time to recognize unique contributions made by regiments in the British army. BBC's Frank Gillard marked the contribution made by the 3rd Tank Regiment from France in 1940 through the war in the North African desert, Greece, Crete, with the Eighth Army at El Alamein and D-Day. Hampshire was well-represented in this regiment. Hampshire men were also making distinguished contributions to the Medium Regiment, Royal Artillery or the Gunners. By the first months of 1945 they were well inside Germany. They had also played a noteworthy part in the

Sicilian campaign. After D-Day the regiment fired 1,800 tons of ammunition in Normandy in six weeks and was a spearhead in the Second Army's push through Belgium and Holland. On New Year's Day 1945 they were moving to throw back Von Rundstedt's offensive with Canadian troops. Lieutenant John Pragnell who was serving with the 50th Northumberland Division 'Monty's Own' hailed from Hampshire and was also involved in responding to the German attack called the Battle of the Bulge. He was 22 years old and had joined the army in 1941. He had trained at Sandhurst and was commissioned at a ceremony on 11 March when General Eisenhower took the salute. Individual sacrifice was exemplified by Paratrooper Peter Griffiths who was just 19 when he parachuted into Arnhem where he was taken prisoner after being severely wounded. His left leg was amputated in a German hospital. At the age of 15 he had joined the Aldershot Home Guard and in 1941 joined the army and was fighting in Egypt by the time he was 17. He went on to fight in Italy and returned to Britain to prepare for D-Day. However, death did not take only those on active service, as in the case of Sub-Lieutenant Reginald Foulstone who was killed in a training accident in Texas and who had recently earned his wings. He had been a draftsman at the RAE and had served in the Aldershot Home Guard before volunteering for the Fleet Air Arm. He was aged 22. Local Ash Green man Bombardier Leonard Summers was saluted in the *Aldershot News* as a Chindit – sometimes referred to as the 'Forgotten Army' – for action in Burma, resulting in his award of the Military Medal. He had been part of the 14th Army in India and Burma for four years after serving in the force defending Dover. Private Charles Cooper of the Queen's Royal Regiment returned to Aldershot following the liberation of his PoW camp in Germany. He had been in captivity for five years and had been involved in the 'death march' across Germany until being liberated by American forces. In a similar way, Private John Hemmings, also of the Queen's Royal Regiment, announced his arrival back home after being captured in France on 20 May 1940 with a loud knock on his family's door in Aldershot.

Speaking in Aldershot, South African Flight Lieutenant Stewart, DFC, a veteran of forty-four bombing raids over Germany as a bomb-aimer in Lancasters, described his experience. He and his brother had come to Britain in 1940 to serve in her hour of need. His brother had been killed in the Battle of Britain when his Spitfire was brought down. Flight Lieutenant Stewart's most recent mission had been to Peenemünde, the location for development and production of V-1 and V-2 rockets:

> We ran into trouble when two Fw 190s came in beneath us. Our rear gunner was hit and they returned and shot up our rear outer engine, setting the plane on fire. We managed to put the fires out but we were a sitting target. Fortunately we were not attacked again and managed to get the plane back, having to make a belly-landing because our wheels had

jammed. Our rear gunner died in hospital but not before enquiring if he had 'let the crew down.'

On a raid on the Skoda Works, Stewart had to confess that they had bombed a phantom city created by the Germans. Recognition of outstanding war service was not just a male affair, as Leading Wren J.V. Blundell from Aldershot received the British Empire Medal from the king for outstanding work associated with D-Day.

The whole process of rehabilitating returning prisoners of war began in Hampshire. In March 1945 Corporal Thomas O'Brien described a forced march across Germany until he was released by American troops. Repatriated PoWs were entertained in Hampshire boroughs when they began returning in June 1944. In Aldershot the mayor spoke of the 140 temporary houses being built for which they would be given priority. One of the soldiers entertained was Private Cyril Stevens who had been in Stalag 74 since being captured in Italy in October 1944. A similar reception was given to Ash PoWs with Mr A. Scard, whose son, a PoW, describing the work of a local committee sending food parcels throughout the war. After three and a half years in Germany, Quartermaster Sergeant Walter Barr had returned to Tongham. He joined the RAMC based at the Cambridge Hospital in 1920 and had been taken prisoner at St Omer in 1940 serving with the BEF. He eventually ended up in Poland where he reported that he and his fellow PoWs had been poorly clad and poorly fed. Few Red Cross parcels had reached them. In response to their guards claiming that British towns had been destroyed, they delighted in producing letters from towns their guards claimed had been wiped out. However, they had been largely left to themselves and had organized plays and concerts of a high standard. Hampshire was the location for a dispersal camp for 1,200 PoWs and there was a unanimous view that it was the Red Cross parcels that had kept them alive. Decent hot food was given to the men, as well as music and cinema. The men maintained that they could not have survived on the rations provided by the Germans and were very grateful to the Red Cross. There were seventeen Australians who had been captured in Greece and sent to Poland where they suffered considerably, enduring temperatures that fell to 42 degrees below zero. Hubert Storey-Day, an Aldershot man recently repatriated, was an example of a civilian caught in France when German troops overran the country in 1940. He was allowed to go back to his house to collect rations for three days before he was taken to barracks in Lille. After five days he was taken to a fortress at Huy overlooking the River Meuse. On 9 September 1940 he was transported to a camp in Upper Silesia 500ft up in the Vosges Mountains. At first food was in very short supply but on 25 February the camp began to receive Red Cross parcels. Civilian prisoners of war were made to work but left to their own devices for much of the time and later in the war cheered American bombers when they flew overhead.

One of the canteens given by donations from the Commonwealth to Hampshire towns.

Signing the Freedom of the Borough of Aldershot by the mayor.

The 1st Division of the Hampshire Regiment receiving the Freedom of the Borough of Aldershot, September 1944.

Members of Gale & Polden, Aldershot's prize-winning fire protection service.

Admiral Lane in Aldershot for Support the Navy Week.

Hampshire soldiers fighting in Sicily in 1943.

Hampshire Fire and Rescue Service demonstrate their wartime capability.

Support the Navy Week parade in Aldershot.

Air-raid wardens march on parade.

Regimental parade in Hampshire.

GIs helping to entertain children in wartime.

Recuperating members of the armed forces at Park Prewett Hospital, Basingstoke.

Inspecting a new tank in Hampshire.

Three Aldershot soldiers overseas.

With hundreds of Hampshire men and women putting their lives on the line in combat zones there was little tolerance shown to those whom it was felt were not pulling their weight in factories associated with the war effort. An RAE toolmaker who overslept after two years of working on night shifts received a £4.00 fine, while another RAE stoker with bad timekeeping was sent to prison. Whether these punishments were a result of emulating Soviet ideas from contact with a Soviet army officer who spoke to the Aldershot Anglo-Soviet Committee in Aldershot could be a possibility. What was more important to most people was the arrival of more supplies of coal in Hampshire towns during February.

Support Warship Week in Aldershot.

Pantomime to support a local Hampshire hospital.

CHAPTER TWENTY-FIVE

The Hampshire Regiment

During the Second World War the Hampshire Regiment had six battalions on active service abroad and in Britain. The battalions that fought abroad were the 1st, 2nd, 1/4th, 5th and 7th, while the 50th Holding Battalion moved around bases in the United Kingdom. The Holding Battalion was based on the Isle of Wight at the commencement of the war carrying out training activities for 50 officers and 1,200 other ranks. However, it moved back to Bournemouth in 1939 to operate among the holidaymakers there. By 11 November 1939 the battalion was at Parkhurst on the Isle of Wight at the Albany Barracks defending Sandown Beach where they were training with the commandos. Further moves took it to Colchester and Northern Ireland. In June 1944, prior to D-Day, they assembled in a marshalling area in Portsmouth from whence they were disbanded.

The 70th Battalion was based in Southampton from 26 April 1940 with the emphasis being on 'young soldiers'. They were then moved to Basingstoke with a specific duty to protect the airfields of Middle Wallop, Worthy Down, Chilbolton and Ibsley, a role that was subsequently taken over by the Royal Air Force Regiment. On 1 October they were designated as a counter-attack regiment then being moved to Bridport as a training unit. The efficient operation of the Hampshires was dependent on the Depot Battalion responsible for management of the disparate activities in which the Hampshires were engaged. This work started in 1938.

With the threat of invasion in October 1940, the Hampshires became a field force. In November 1940 the battalion moved to Bournemouth where it was employed in building scaffolding around the town's beaches. Then in March 1941 it was moved to Lyndhurst where it was given a major role in training.

Total loss of life for the Hampshires during the war was 2,094 officers and men. In examining the elements making up the Hampshires it is necessary to look at the 1st Battalion whose men were regular soldiers and whose experience of the war reads like a Cook's tour of the combat zones. The opening weeks of the war found them carrying out garrison duties at El Daba in Egypt. They moved to Palestine in December 1939 and from there to three bases in Egypt in the summer of 1940. In February 1941 they were moved to Malta where their men were involved in airfield repair and as stevedores on the docks and experienced the siege of the island at first hand. By April

1943 they were in Alexandria training as an independent assault brigade in preparation for the invasion of Sicily where they were to suffer 18 officers and 286 other ranks killed. On 8 September 1943, the 231st Brigade came ashore at Porto San Venere near Pizzo in Italy, being withdrawn in October 1943 to return to the UK for the first time in twenty-three years. On 11 November 1943 they commenced training for D-Day at Long Melford near Sudbury. This was followed from February by further training at Castlelands Park near Southampton, Lyndhurst and Beaulieu.

D-Day was being planned using new weapons such as flail tanks, while Scorpions and Crocodile assault vehicles were being tested. Rehearsed landings took place at Studland Bay and Hayling Island called Smash Two and Four. The Hampshire Battalion was allocated to the 50th Northumberland Infantry Division prior to D-Day. Before the battalion was sealed in their camp on the day before D-Day, there was a march past that featured many men drawn from Hampshire. The two landing craft they were on were the HMS *Empire Arquebus* and SS *Empire Broadsword*. Denis Hawn remembered the crossing from Lymington to his designated beach as being unpleasant but uneventful. A deserter had been apprehended just before they left and he was wearing ordinary shoes. His landing craft was hit and its bridge destroyed. He and three companions jumped into the sea but he was the only one who made the shore and because of this he believes the others were never recorded as having been killed in the landing and there is no memorial to them. Around him there were landing craft exploding on mines and waxen corpses floating in the water, while on the beach medics were beginning to treat ghastly wounds. They had landed in France on 6 June 1944 when they were on the right of the initial assault on SWORD Beach. The rough sea they encountered placed the whole landing in jeopardy with only two of the sixteen landing craft of which they were part making the shore. The flail tanks required to clear mines bogged down and the bombers and fire from naval vessels had failed to destroy the bunkered gun emplacements along the beach. As the first men ashore with little support, it was only the effective training the Hampshires had been put through that carried them through to a successful landing. Despite this, they captured Le Hamel and Arromanches after a landing carried out without the assistance of tanks and in the face of machine-gun fire. Their casualties were 182 with 64 killed in action. There then followed a whole series of hard-fought battles until on 31 August the 31st Battalion crossed the Seine and entered Amiens. Its command then switched to the Guards Armoured Division and was involved in attempts to relieve the trapped British and Polish troops after Arnhem. Since D-Day the 1st Battalion Hampshire Regiment suffered more than 1,281 casualties including 231 officers and men killed in action.

Like the 1st Battalion, the 2nd Battalion started the war as part of the regular army. It was based in Aldershot and in September 1939 moved to Cherbourg with the 1st Guards Brigade accompanied by the 3rd Battalion

Grenadier Guards and 2nd Battalion Coldstream Guards attached to the 1st Infantry Division. By February 1940 they were on the Belgian/French border interrupted by three weeks on the Maginot Line. On 16 May the battalion began its retreat to Dunkirk, managing to retain all of their small arms. Ben Duncan, who was born in Ryde, joined the army at the age of 19 in 1936 and the Hampshire Regiment became his entire life till he retired in 1972. His memory of the Dunkirk retreat was of the hundreds of miles of walking involved. For the ordinary soldier the extent of the defeat only became recognizable when Dunkirk was reached. 'All Hampshire Regiment this way,' was announced on a loudhailer and they clambered onto a jetty. His friend was injured and had to be helped to climb the ladder from the small boat to the destroyer. Waiting for them on board was a blessed cup of tea and a bully beef sandwich. He was carrying his Bren gun so was asked to go back as the Germans had broken through into the town. He said he was not able to follow the order because the gun was jammed. Fortunately someone else volunteered. Jim Goodall from Alton characterized the whole experience of the Hampshires in France as operating with unfamiliar weapons in an untrained manner. They were then designated for home defence for the following two years. In November 1942 the Hampshire Regiment formed part of Operation TORCH with the 1st Guards Brigade in the 78th Infantry Division landing in Algiers on 21 November. On 1 December they moved to Teboura where they were attacked by a force four times their size. On 3 December 1942 Major Wallace Le Patourel won the Victoria Cross by leading bayonet counter-attacks with four volunteers from his regiment. The task was to silence a machine gun on the top of a hill overlooking them. When his three companions were killed he went forward alone with a revolver and grenades and silenced it himself. Having started the battle with 689 men, the battalion had been reduced to just 194.

The Hampshire Battalion came to include men from the Territorial Army which was doubled in 1939 following a campaign of recruitment. Men from the various battalions recruited were grouped into the 128th Infantry Brigade and the 130th Brigade, both being part of the 43rd Wessex Infantry Division. The 128th Brigade was sent to North Africa as part of Operation TORCH, landing in Algiers on 17 January. They were involved in heavy fighting through to the beginning of March when they were relieved by the Argyll and Sutherland Highlanders. They lost 243 men killed or missing. With the fall of Tunis in May 1943, the 128th was part of the assault landing group at Salerno under the command of the US army. W. Bowden remembered wading through waist-high water with his rifle over his head and a wireless strapped to his chest. They had an objective of getting 6 miles inland but the landings were something of a disaster because they had been put onto the wrong beach. He was left with a despondent feeling after being captured by the Germans in an ambush. During the Italian fighting the 128th suffered 1,276 casualties.

In May 1944 an element of the 128th was involved in the assault on Monte Cassino and during this fighting Captain Robert Wakeford was awarded the Victoria Cross. After being wounded in the face and arms he led a charge up a hill in order to take out a machine gun. At Montegridolfo Lieutenant G.R. Norton won the Hampshires' third VC by showing 'matchless courage' in mounting an attack on a machine-gun position incurring severe wounds to his legs. In an amazing coincidence, when he was taken to hospital he discovered that his nurse was his twin sister. On 22 November they were in action to capture a bridgehead over the River Cosina, this being their last action in Italy. They were then flown to Greece to put down an attack by ELAS (the Greek People's Liberation Army) whom they had trained and who were now seeking to overthrow the Greek government, changing their name to 'Tiger Force'. Arriving on 17 February 1945, it was not until April 1945 that ELAS was finally disbanded. The element of the Hampshires that had been left in Italy ended their war at Forli, northern Italy on VE Day. On 15 May they were on the Austrian/Yugoslavian border, later being transferred to Vienna on garrison duties in the British zone of the city.

The 7th Battalion, a Territorial Army unit, was split into the 5th and 7th battalions and remained in the UK preparing for the D-Day landing at Le Hamel (GOLD) beach in June 1944 as part of Operation OVERLORD. In July they were confronted by a crack regiment of the Waffen-SS supported by Tiger tanks and suffered casualties of 18 officers and 208 other ranks with 4 officers and 12 other ranks being killed. By August the 7th Battalion was preparing for the 'break-out' from northern France and on 27 August the battalion crossed the River Seine. At this stage since they landed in Normandy they had lost 35 officers and 450 other ranks (including wounded). On 19 December when the Germans launched their Battle of the Bulge Ardennes offensive they moved into position north of Liège to guard bridges over the Meuse. By 26 March they had crossed the Rhine and began sweeping through Germany, encountering minimal resistance. Prior to the surrender of the Germans on 3 May they had to deal with hundreds of PoWs.

A 9th Battalion of the Hampshires was formed on the Isle of Wight in July 1940 but after it was transferred to other brigades it was broken up in August 1943. A 10th Battalion was created in July 1940 in Aldershot with a feature being the naming of its individual tanks following combat as part of the Hampshire Regiment. It served with distinction as part of the 34th Tank Brigade at Le Havre, Reichswald Forest and in Operation PLUNDER from 1944 to 1945. A 70th Young Soldiers' Battalion was formed in September 1940 and moved to Basingstoke. It consisted of soldiers in the 18 to 19 age group who could not be conscripted. It was disbanded when the government lowered the age of conscription to 18.

On 16 September 1945 at the Aldershot recreation ground full tribute was paid to the Hampshire Regiment and the sacrifice made by its men during the war. The detachments representing the borough were 1st and 4th brigade Major R.L. Elwin; Captain W. Perin King's Colour; Captain H.F. Wright Regimental Colour; 2nd and 4th divisions Captain T.A. Baker; Captain F.J. Barker; Lieutenant L.H. Dees 14th Holding (3rd Battalion Colours); 5th Battalion detachment Major P. Ayers; Lieutenant L.C. Sherwood King's Colours; Lieutenant G.A.F. Minnigin DCM, MM, King's Colours; 7th Battalion Captain F.P. Hillman King's Colours; Captain J. Williams Regimental Colour; and R.S.M. Ware (Command Detachment). The regimental band of the Hampshires accompanied the entry of the troops and Aldershot's mayoral party in their civic robes. Onlookers cheered in the West Stand as the troops marched past them and the mayor and Lieutenant Colonel J.M. Lee DSO took the salute. After a formal address setting out the way in which the Hampshires had contributed to the war effort, a scroll conferring the Freedom of Aldershot was handed over. On the Tuesday morning of the presentation the men of the Hampshires had arrived in town and marched to the parade ground through streets of cheering crowds and houses bedecked with flags. Local members of the British Legion were recognized when flags were dipped as a mark of their service in previous wars. F.S. George in commenting said that the qualities exemplified by the Hampshires should provide an inspiration for the people of Aldershot towards promoting the peace of the world. He said that in no way was the pageantry a glorification of war.

CHAPTER TWENTY-SIX

Hampshire Celebrates Victory in Europe

With the arrival of May 1945 the weather turned for the better as if the war's end had been foreseen. The news was that the Allies were at the gates of Berlin, so optimism was in the warm air. German surrender took place and Churchill designated 8 May as VE Day announced with ships' hooters and sirens sounding loudly in Portsmouth Harbour. The UK's special relationship with the United States was shown by the mixture of union flags and the stars and stripes throughout Hampshire. Young women wore ribbons celebrating the victory in their hair and red, white and blue outfits. The dockyards at Southampton and Portsmouth had fallen silent and for housewives the never-ending queues seemed almost bearable. However, the Portsmouth Women Citizens' Association criticized the constant queuing for almost every sort of food as a terrible tax on women's lives. Although it was still in ruins, crowds in Portsmouth gravitated towards its Guildhall to participate in a service of thanksgiving and these were also taking place throughout the county. Some of the celebrations involved the burning of effigies of Hitler. Spontaneous street parties took place, many utilizing foodstuffs hoarded during the years of the war. Almost from nowhere musical instruments and musicians to play them would appear. In Portsmouth, with complete disregard for safety, some revellers climbed into the Guildhall bell tower and attempted to ring its bell. Despite injunctions against bonfires, wood from the numerous bomb sites was thrown onto the bonfires lit in parts of Hampshire, some growing to such a size that they worried the Hampshire authorities. With the fine weather, crowds were flocking to Southsea and the WRNS from Stockheath shed their uniforms to sunbathe on Hayling Island.

Sheila Foy described how their street party in Moen Road came to pass. Those who could not contribute money for the party found jellies and tinned fruit from their cupboards. Tables were brought out from houses and in the absence of tablecloths crepe paper was used. Someone had an old wind-up record player and some 78rpm records for dancing. Despite heavy work commitments, some men who were not in the services managed to come to the party. Fortunately it was a warm night so the celebrations were able to go on well past midnight. Bunting and flags were borrowed from nearby naval barracks. Sheila remembered that they could not open their windows because flags were jammed in them. Paper hats were constructed out of newspaper.

VE Day street party with servicemen.

The following morning they had to have breakfast on the floor as the tables were still out in the street. However, Eric Haynes remembered his VE Day anchored off Portsmouth and making preparations to travel to the East for the campaign against Japan. Canadian bandsman Norman Gibson recalled playing at VE Day celebrations but pointed out that shortly afterwards the Canadians began winding down military bands in Britain.

Singer Brenda Logic said:

> I was doing my army show in the Avenue Hall (Southampton) and suddenly an officer came on to the stage. Everyone started jeering and telling him to get off but he calmed them down by saying he had something to tell them. He then said that the war was over. Some laughed. Some cried. Most didn't know what to do. Then the whole place erupted. The show I was doing was abandoned and instead we just sang and sang. The whole hall broke into *There'll Always be an England* and *Land of Hope and Glory*.

On Tuesday, 8 May American Jeeps and lorries toured Southampton with their horns blaring. Doreen Bowers remembered 'an immense feeling of relief to sleep at night knowing there would be no air-raids or sounds of gunfire or bombs exploding…' She noted that not everyone wanted to join in the celebrations because they were still in mourning for the loss of loved ones and had no cause to celebrate. On VE Day she was in London shouting for the king and Winston Churchill. As she and her friend were walking past Downing Street, Churchill's car passed them and he waved and gave a victory sign. In Newport, Isle of Wight, when the news came that the war was over it was as if a carnival had been announced and almost miraculously bunting appeared everywhere. In Ryde, workmen hung bunting across the High Street to such an extent that the street became a mass of flowing colours. Cowes chose to highlight the remembrance of its past regatta glories by dressing the vessels in its harbour in the brightest of colours.

A member of the Hampshires, Donald 'Dixie' Dean, remembered the end of the war coming when he was in Italy where fighting ceased on 2 May and climbing into a fountain in Rome to celebrate after a session of heavy drinking. He was in the middle of parachute training 10 miles from Rome. In Aldershot, the *Aldershot Borough and Fleet Times* signalled the administrative arrangements for the cessation of hostilities on 6 April 1945. Three days' holiday was announced for all government establishments, one on the day of the announcement and two others on another date. However, there was no holiday for those working in essential services such as gas and electricity. On Wednesday, 4 April Aldershot Council considered what celebrations might be organized in the camp and town to mark the peace. Councillors were concerned that unless plans were made in advance of the official announcement of Germany's surrender, Aldershot would lose the prominence it should enjoy. In the end the council's Welcome Home Committee was given responsibility for arrangements. In Farnborough councillors believed that an open-air ceremony of thanksgiving should take place by 4 May and detailed arrangements for the celebrations to follow were being put in place to mark the collapse of German aggression that had kept the world in agony for five years. Reported was the suicide of Hitler, the surrender of German troops in Italy and the surrender of the Germans in Berlin. Also reported was how Germany would now stand at the bar of justice for all the sorrow, misery and destruction inflicted on the world. The Home Office suggested that at the king's wish, the celebrations for VE Day should be held on the first Sunday after that day.

Cinemas and dance halls were given permission by councils to remain open longer than usual on any day marking VE Day and in Aldershot the garrison churches should give thanksgiving services as with churches of all denominations. It was expected that in the borough there would be a parade of more than 4,000 military, civil and pre-service units that would assemble at 8.30 am and march through the High Street to reach the recreation ground at 9.30

am where local clergy and army chaplains would conduct the service. When the service was over the assembled units would march past the commander of the Aldershot Military District, Major General H.O. Curtis. This duly took place on 11 May. Aldershot's MP, the Rt Hon. Oliver Lyttelton, sent a special 'Peace Message' to his constituents, stating that VE Day was the 'greatest moment in the country's history' due to the defeat of Germany on her own soil by Allied forces. The victory had been won against a fanatical and barbarous enemy who had been unhampered by any thoughts of humanity towards the unfortunate people oppressed by Germany. He gave his congratulations to all in the country including the armed forces, civil defence, the workers in the factories and workers on the farms who had made up the gap in food supplies curtailed by submarine attacks. A crucial element in the message was the recognition of how British women had maintained households, however grim the circumstances throughout the war. To Aldershot he gave the credit for providing the basis for the rapid advance of the Allied army into Germany to finish the war.

Mayor of Aldershot, J.W. White JP, in his address for VE Day recognized Aldershot's fortune in escaping the worst of the bombing but also recognized the ceaseless work of civil defence organizations. Importantly he identified those in the community unable to celebrate the end of the war because they were still mourning the loss of loved ones. Although the local fire service was not called upon to deal with local incendiary bombs, they were called upon to deal with huge fires in Portsmouth and London. He praised the town for the way in which it had supported the weeks of intensive fund-raising such as Warships Week, Weapons Week, Wings for Victory, Salute the Soldier, Merchant Navy Week and Spitfire Week. Major General H.O. Curtis, commander of the Aldershot and Hampshire District, congratulated the town on its role as the spearhead of the British Expeditionary Force deeply involved with the military and civilian population prior to 1939 and its dispatch to France. He recognized the crucial role played by the Home Guard in freeing the army for combat abroad. In Farnborough a similar march through the centre of the town and an assembly at the playing fields were organized.

Mr W.H.T. Cunnington MBE, JP, CC, chairman of Farnborough Urban Council, noted that for the first time civilians had been in the front line of battle. He pointed out their crucial role in achieving victory. Where there had been air-raids in Farnborough, civil defence and post-raid services had acted very efficiently. There was praise for the support that the Farnborough community had offered to members of the fighting services billeted upon them. He praised the role played by 'our' regiment, the Hampshires, in Africa, Italy and in Germany.

Wanda Goolen, a member of the Women's Land Army from Southampton, spoke of the honour of representing Hampshire at the Victory Parade in London on 8 May. The train to London was so crowded that she had to stand all the way. All the Land Girls were invited to a lavish tea at the Land Army Club and were billeted at the Royal Palace Hotel in Kensington.

On the Saturday morning they were formed up in lines twelve abreast and then marched behind the women of the WVS through Hyde Park to Marble Arch and on to Oxford Street where the cheering was so loud that they could not hear the band behind them. The day ended with viewing the fireworks from Westminster Bridge. In Church Crookham Peter Silvester remembered attending a VE party for local children. He was aged 10 and his sister who went with him was 12. 'It was amazing what lovely food and treats they managed to muster up considering the shortage of food in 1945,' he said.

On 26 September 1945, three years after the failed raid on Dieppe, Aldershot held a Drumhead Service to mark the Second World War victory at the recreation ground in Aldershot. It was the first time that a complete army had been granted the Freedom of the Borough. Squadron Leader James Dunn of the Royal Canadian Air Force, in a letter to Aldershot Council, said he was 'Delighted. The heaping of such coals of fire humbles and honours us and provides for us yet another instance for admiration of England and the English.' The arrival of 10,000 marching Canadians, many from the 2nd Canadian Special Infantry Battalion based on Old Dean Common, Camberley, was accompanied by the Canadian Military Band. In the scroll given to the Canadian commander, the Honourable P.J. Montague CB, CG, DSO, MC by the mayor of Aldershot, mention is made of the long history of Canadian sacrifice from Vimy Ridge, Passchendaele, Ypres, Dieppe, Ortona, Ravenna, Falaise and Nijmegen. In his speech after the receipt of the scroll, General Montague spoke about how during the war Aldershot had been the centre of their life and how they had been a 'good, happy family'. He mentioned the many marriages arising from the presence of Canadian troops in the Aldershot community, and concluded: 'We give you this assurance that as long as the winds blow and the rivers run in Canada we will remain loyal to this Mother Country and we shall never forget Aldershot.' On the following Sunday at Aldershot's Baptists' Tabernacle the Canadian Chaplaincy Service was granted the Freedom of the Church. On their return to Canada, with rationing still in operation, a consignment of scarce foodstuffs was sent for the families most in need in the borough. For the local girls carried off by the Canadians, what of their fate? Two sisters – Violet and Edie Jessiman – married Canadians they had met at a dance in Aldershot. Violet settled in Manitoba and Violet in Alberta. Many of these war brides crossed the Atlantic to their spouses on the *Queen Mary* which they described as a 'floating palace' because after the grim reality of rationing they encountered food that they had almost forgotten ever existed. Some had babies with them and Edith Gardner described the assistance given to them by the Red Cross. Her destination was a small town in Ontario where she was greeted in a friendly way. However, not all the experiences were positive ones with some reports of parents having to send money for their daughters to return home due to the unsatisfactory circumstances that awaited them in Canada. It is sad to report the fate of some local brides who never received the invitation to join their husbands in Canada, and many children with Canadian fathers who never even saw them.

VE Day street party.

Street party for VE Day in Hampshire.

CHAPTER TWENTY-SEVEN

On to VJ Day

Frank Colenso, speaking at the FAST (Farnborough Air Sciences Trust) museum, spoke about his recollections of VJ Day on 15 August 1945. He was in the RAF at Toungoo airfield in Rangoon, Burma working as an airframe fitter with the 3rd Repair and Salvage Unit supporting 155 Squadron. In the morning Spitfires continued to bomb the Japanese army returning from twenty-minute flights to rearm and refuel. 'Beside the airfield a battery from the Royal Artillery kept up a deafening bombardment into the hills, only pausing to allow our Spitfires to land and then the silence was awesome – not a sound was heard – leaving me with a dawning realisation that at last the war was over.' An excessive amount of food became available, together with the rum ration. It was not until 1947 that Mr Colenso returned to the UK as his unit was chosen as the British Commonwealth Occupation Force in Japan. After the war he moved to Farnborough where he worked as an airframe fitter at the RAE.

Elizabeth Goneau worked in signals and was in Aldershot on VJ Day. Possibly because of the disruption caused by the Canadian riot in the town, she was confined to barracks. In Aldershot the council decided that the VJ Day celebrations would include two days of dances, fireworks, floodlights and a united service of thanksgiving. The government decreed two days of holiday and at midday shops and businesses were closed. Although flags and decorations seemed to appear from nowhere, rain in the period prior to midday seemed to dampen enthusiasm for the celebration. In the afternoon there was a baseball match at the recreation ground and people danced to the music of a military band. On the following Thursday at the recreation ground at 11.15 am a thanksgiving service was attended by 4,000 members of the armed forces. A similar service was held in Farnborough at its recreation ground where the salute was taken by Brigadier General Gough. Jack Yeatman, a Royal Navy and Royal Air Force wireless operator, expected to be transferred to the East in preparation for an invasion of Japan after VE Day. He had been involved in escorting convoys from the Solent to Welsh ports.

Despite news of the Japanese surrender and the nationwide VJ Day celebrations, there were reports that the final peace after almost six years of conflict came as something of an anti-climax. This may have been due to the interval between victory in Europe and victory in the East; also that great numbers of the armed forces would have a lengthy wait for repatriation to their home countries and reunion with their loved ones.

CHAPTER TWENTY-EIGHT

Aftermath

In order to achieve the peace, Hampshire's exhausted population had had to cope with attack from Hitler's *vergeltungswaffen* reprisal weapons for raids on German cities by Allied bombers. The primitive rocket system of the V-1 and V-2 bombs was located in the missile's tail. There was a terrible uncertainty about these bombs because no siren was sounded indicating that the raid was over. When the V-1 engine cut out, there was a moment of silence while it fell to earth with its four-fifths of explosives falling to earth at 400 miles an hour. By the end of the war some 500 V-1s had been launched, causing 24,000 casualties nationwide. The last V-1 rocket fell on 29 March 1945, reflecting the advance of Allied troops overrunning the launch sites. As the Hampshires moved into Germany they discovered the true horror of the Nazi regime in the concentration camps that they liberated.

Public opinion-polling at this time revealed that the British blamed Hitler's regime and not the German people, evidence that this nation was not good at hating other people. What the *Picture Post* reflected at this time was a greater concern for shaping the post-war world. For working people in Hampshire, memories of what had happened after the Great War were an important factor. Symbolic of this were old ex-soldiers seeking to sell vacuum cleaners and other items door-to-door in Southampton and Aldershot. The lingering image for poorer families in Hampshire of the world prior to 1939 was one of means-testing when work disappeared. The demand now was for work for all, health for all and a better education for all. These demands were based on the findings of reports written during the war by William Beveridge on employment and community support and Richard Butler on education. Councils such as that of Aldershot began considering their educational provision in the light of Butler's recommendations, such as making secondary education available to all children. Even before the war, the British Medical Association was advocating a National Health Service and now it became an important part of the platform for social change. Hampshire councils began to look at premises that might be occupied by National Health Service hospitals. Sometimes, paradoxically, this might be an old workhouse.

The assumption that when the war ended the old pre-war certainties of life would return were demolished by the election that took place between VE and VJ Day and highlighted in by-elections. The Labour leader Clement Attlee had decided that after victory in Europe coalition government should come

GI brides on their way to America.

German submarine surrendering in Portsmouth.

to an end and normal democracy should be reinstated. After all, there had not been a proper general election since 1935. On 6 July in Portsmouth, the Lord Mayor announced the results for Portsmouth's three constituencies. Although voters had gone to the polls on 25 June, the result throughout Hampshire was delayed until the votes of men serving overseas had been counted. It is widely accepted that those votes, often shaped by near-death experiences, had prompted a demand for radical change in the country for which they had fought. Throughout Hampshire the political landscape changed radically. In Portsmouth South, Labour came within 3,027 votes of taking the seat. In 1935 the Conservative majority had been 18,373. Portsmouth Central saw Labour overturning a Conservative majority of 10,733 and taking the seat, and in Portsmouth North Labour overturned a Conservative majority of 11,454. Labour did not contest Aldershot but Tom Wintringham stood against the sitting MP, the Rt Hon. Oliver Lyttelton, as a candidate for the Common Wealth Party (a socialist party formed in 1942). His policies advocated building on the reality of wartime state ownership of many parts of the economy to create a fairer distribution of wealth in Britain. This idea must have found favour in Aldershot because the Conservative majority shrank from 11,315 in 1935 to 5,023 in 1945, despite Lyttelton lauding the roles of Churchill and Eden as wartime leaders throughout the Aldershot constituency. At council level in November 1945, in Portsmouth Labour gained nine seats and the Communist Party one seat, producing a council chamber with Labour members seated on the left for the first time. The establishment manifested by the Archbishop of Canterbury and *The Times* believed that the sacrifice made during the war should be rewarded by greater equality in the country.

This was a war that brought geopolitical change as well as social change to Hampshire. The call of Empire that had brought thousands of Canadians to the county would no longer hold sway as it had done in both world wars. The British connection was weakened as Canada would now look more to her American neighbour for support in the subsequent Cold War with the Soviet Union. Immediately Britain was beset by economic problems necessitating cuts in her armed forces which had a direct effect on Hampshire's manufacturing base because of its relation to war production. Hampshire farmers now benefited from agricultural protection but the pre-war role of Canada as Britain's bread-basket diminished because of it.

In Hampshire, as with the rest of the country, the salient question was how now to win the peace? In September, Prime Minister Clement Attlee told the Trades Union Conference of 1945 that all he could offer was hard work and patience towards the austerity faced by the country. Rationing and shortages had bred an alternative black market system such as the flooding of the country with fake petrol coupons. The switch from wartime habits did not always go smoothly. On 22 August, Major Sir Jocelyn Lucas, MP for Portsmouth South, speaking in the House of Commons, complained to the

First Lord of the Admiralty that the dockyards were still using the air-raid sirens that brought back terrible memories to those in the surrounding area. He was assured that 'moaning Minnie' (as it was called) would be replaced by a factory hooter. A more serious reminder of the war years were the mines washed ashore in October gales in the Portsmouth area and along the coast from Hastings to the Devon border. HMS *Vernon* had her work cut out in trying to cope with them. Fortunately the explosions that occurred were usually on uninhabited beaches but one explosion was severe enough to break windows in Freshwater and Yarmouth on the Isle of Wight. A police sergeant and a constable, knowing that the bomb disposal teams from HMS *Vernon* were under tremendous pressure, exploded three mines that were on Hayling Island. In the end the Portsmouth Command had to deal with almost 100 mines, of which 20 required detonation.

Inland may have been more peaceful but it did not escape a first-hand reminder of the war when in November 200 child refugees from Belsen arrived in Durley, near Bishop's Waltham. There were some among them whose only experience was of growing up in a concentration camp and they bore the physical and mental scars of their earlier life. A place was found for them at the former wartime headquarters of the National Fire Service at Wintershill Hall, Durley. On a drizzling morning in November, HMS *Nelson*, crewed entirely by men from Portsmouth, arrived back from the Far East to the sound of the Royal Marine Band on the railway jetty marking her arrival.

Mindful of the world of rationing to which they were returning, oranges and bananas were thrown to waiting children. One saucy sailor waved a pair of silk panties, aware that they represented the epitome of luxury to austerity Portsmouth. The people of South Africa, conscious of the suffering of people in the bombed-out areas of Portsmouth, Gosport and Southampton, donated 1,344 plum puddings for Christmas 1945. Unfortunately bad weather delayed the cargo's arrival. To this disappointment was added a coal shortage, making for a bleak festival season as gales lashed the south coast. These gales also meant that the Isle of Wight became isolated because the ferries could not sail. As a result, 1,400 people slept either on trains or on a ferry. The one glimmer of light was the arrival of the first cargo of bananas since 1940.

More important historically is the wartime archaeology to be found in places around Southampton such as the pill-boxes around the Hamble airfield and Chamberlain Hall in Glen Eyre Road. Further, the tank traps in the recreation ground at Upper Shirley can be pointed out. Where once stood the Ordnance Survey Building behind the Law Courts is now a car park. Around the coast are the slipways crucial to D-Day and at Lepe beach the foundations for the Mulberry harbour.

The Canadian army had to devise ways to keep its servicemen occupied while here because of the slow pace of repatriation to Canada. One of these was a Christmas show called the Rhythm Rodeo along the lines of Colonel

Oliver Lyttelton, MP for Aldershot, whose majority was slashed in the 1945 General Election.

Cody's travelling rodeo of the 1890s. The show aimed to reproduce all the elements of the original with shooting, Red Indians, wagons and barn-dancing and was located in the grounds of a manor house at Peper Harow in Surrey, just off the A3. On 15 December 1945 it premièred with a cast of 400 representing great efforts to produce authenticity with horses shipped from Ireland, frontier saddles sent over from Canada and 150 cast members drawn from all ranks in the Canadian army. Producing and directing the show was the English-born Commanding Officer of Canadian Army Shows, Lieutenant Colonel Rai Purdy, who in civilian life had been an actor, writer, showman and producer. Colonel Purdy was able to draw on talented staff such as Anna Sweeney who devised the dancing and George Simpson who was the show's designer. Included in the show were a stagecoach hold-up, simulated swimming girls in a blue, yellow and green light display to Gershwin's music, a chariot race, a chuck-wagon race and a snow fantasy. The high point of the show was a re-enactment of the Calgary stampede when riding, lassoing and shooting skills were on display. In the midst of the grey austerity that followed VJ Day, the show provided colour and life for Hampshire residents and the soldiers who had been brought in from repatriation camps.

However, of greatest importance is the emotional remembrance of wartime Southampton. Dora Caton says:

> I think those of us who lived through the war years in a place like Southampton are better equipped to cope with life today than people who are younger. We had to learn to go without food and clothes and household items. We learned to appreciate the daylight hours and nights that were quiet and without fear. We learned how rich life can be and how rewarding it is to care and share with others. My only regret looking back is the loss of family and friends, not of material things, and I am sure we should all join in the prayer 'Let there be peace in our time.'

Bibliography

Primary Sources

Friends of New Forest Airfields

Hampshire Within Living Memory (Hampshire Federation of Women's Institute)

Memories of Basingstoke (True North Books Ltd, 2000)

The Blitz: The Unofficial Story

Ashworth, Chris & Stephens, Patrick, *Action Stations* (The Enthusiast's Publisher)

Barnett, G.E. & Blanchard, V., *City of Portsmouth Records of Corporation 1936–1945* (Her Majesty's Printers, 1965)

Beevor, Anthony, *D-Day: The Battle for Normandy* (Penguin, 2010)

Bissell, Andrew, *Southampton's Children of the Blitz* (Red Post Books, 2001)

Brice, Martin H., Gosling, Nicola & Cross, Tony, *Hampshire's War* (Hampshire Record Office)

Brooks, Robin J., *Hampshire Airfields in the Second World War* (Countryside Books, 1996)

Brown, Malcolm, *Spitfire Gunner*

Burton, Lesley, *Gosport Goes to War, 1939–1945* (Portsmouth News Group, 1981)

Currant, Wing Commander C.F., *So Much Sadness, So Much Fun: RAF Ibsley 1941–1952* (The RAF Historical Group, 1997)

Denis, Commander, *It Was D-Day* (Penguin New Writing, 1945)

Doughty, Martin, *Hampshire and D-Day* (Hampshire Books, 1994)

Fleming, Peter, *Operation Sea Lion* (Simon Schuster, New York, 1957)

Franklin, Claire, Hyslop, Donald & Jemima, Sheila, *Southampton Blitz: The Official Story* (Oral History Team, Southampton Local Studies Section, 1991)

Friend, Douglas J., *Hampshire Boy* (2001)

Gadd, Eric Wyeth, *Hampshire Evacuees* (Paul Cave Publications Ltd, 1982)

Hart-Davis, Duff, *Our Land at War*

Hayward, James, *The Bodies on the Beach: Sea Lion, Shingle Street and the Burning Sea Myth*

Hylton, Stuart, *Reporting the Blitz*

Jenkins, Paul, *Battle over Portsmouth: A City at War, 1940* (Middleton Press, 1986)

Kemp, Anthony, *Southampton at War* (Ensign Publications, 1989)
— *Springboard for Overlord: Hampshire and the D-Day Landings* (Milestone Publications, 1984)
Lamb, Christian, *Redoubtable Wrens at War: Their Trials, Tribulations and Triumphs* (Bene Faction Publishing, 1988)
Lette, John, *In Time of War: Hampshire* (Sutton Publishing Ltd, 2006)
— *The New Forest at War* (Sutton Publishing Ltd, 2004)
Lewis, Peter, *A People's War – A Channel Four Book* (Thames Methuen, 1986)
Lucas, C.E., *Cockleshell Heroes* (Phillips Pan Grand Strategy Series, 1956)
Lunn, Arthur E., *Cove: A Village at War* (Footmark Publications, 1999)
Maclay, Mark, *Aldershot's Canadians in Love and War, 1939–45* (Appin Publications, 1997)
Nash, Stanley Ray, *Recollections of WW2*
Nichols, Virginia, *Millions Like Us* (Viking, 2011)
O'Connell, Geoffrey, *Southwick: The D-Day Village That Went To War* (Ashford Buchan & Enright, 1997)
Osborne, Mike, *Defending Hampshire: The Military Landscape from Prehistory to the Present* (The History Press, 2011)
Pitcher, Anne, *The Cambridge Military Hospital*
Robertson, Kevin, *The Last Days of Steam in Hampshire* (Sutton Publishing, 1987)
Rogo, Joe, *British Military Decline 1919–1939*
Ross, Patricia, *Hampshire at War: An Oral History* (The King's England Press, 2013)
Searle, Adrian, *Isle of Wight 1939–1945* (The Dovecote Press, 1989)
Simons, Colin, *Gramp's War*
Simpkins, Jake, *Southampton in WW2*
Stacey, C.P. & Wilson, Barbara M., *The Half Million: The Canadians in Britain 1939–1946* (University of Toronto Press, 1987)
Webb, J., Quail, S., Haskell, P. & Riley, R., *The Spirit of Portsmouth: A History* (Phillimore, 1989)
White, F.W., *The Story of Gosport*
White, John Baker, *The Big Lie* (Crowell, New York, 1955)
Winton, John, *The Naval Heritage of Portsmouth* (Ensign Publications, 1989)

Secondary Sources

The Aldershot Military Museum
Alton Museum and Archive Centre
The Army Medical Museum
Debbie Reavell, Secretary, Basingstoke Heritage Society
Farnborough and Aldershot Libraries
Gosport History Centre

Hampshire Archives Centre, Winchester
The Hampshire Regiment Museum, Winchester
Lymington Library
Portsmouth History Centre
The Prince Consort Library
Southampton History Centre
The Willis Centre, Basingstoke
Winchester Library and History Centre

Newspapers and Periodicals

'The RAE 1940–1978' (Hugh Warren, *Journal of Aeronautical History*)
'Millions Like Us: Women's lives in War and Peace 1939–1949' (Wendy
    Maddox, *Airspace Magazine*, September 2008)
Aldershot News Group, Gale and Polden, 1939–1946
'How the GI Influx Shaped Britain's View of Americans' (*BBC News
    Magazine*, 24 November 2016)
'Ursula Kantorowicz Arrives at Southampton 2nd February 1939' (*Guardian
    Weekend*, 30 July 2016)
'City at War: A Pictorial Memento of Portsmouth, Gosport, Fareham, Havant
    and Chichester' (Nigel Peak, *Portsmouth News*, 1986)
'The People's War 1939–1940' (Nigel Peak, *Portsmouth News*, 1989)
'Smitten City: The Story of Portsmouth under Blitz' (William G. Easthope,
    Portsmouth News)
'Last British Soldier Home from Dunkirk' (The *Telegraph*, 15 September 2016)

Online Sources

SS *Portsdown*, Daly History Blog, 23 January 2010
Southampton Blitz on Video, Dreamaking, Scarlett Hayler-King, 23 August
    2015
History of Southampton Docks 1940s, YouTube, 23 August 2015

Miscellaneous

American Hospital in Britain Ltd (letter, 3 March 1941)
'Churchill's Navigator John Mitchell', *BBC News*, 11 February 2016
The Connaught Hospital Aldershot 1898–1946, Army Medical Museum,
    Mytchett
D-Day: Our Great Enterprise, Gosport Society
Portsmouth at War, WEA Local History Group, 1983
Royal New Zealand Air Force Museum (details of New Zealand airmen)
The Ventnor Area at War 1939–1945, Ventnor Local History Society

Index